AF556058

Social Change and Development in Medieval Indian History

BY TE SAME AUTHOR

Historiography, Religion and State in Medieval India

Medieval India: From Sultanat to the Mughals—Delhi Sultaat (1206-1526) — Part One

Medieval India: From Sultanat to the Mughals—Mughal Empire (1526-1748) — Part Two

Parties and Politics at the Mughal Court 1707-1740

Social Change and Development in Medieval Indian History

Satish Chandra

HAR-ANAND
PUBLICATIONS PVT LTD

HAR-ANAND PUBLICATIONS PVT LTD
E-49/3, Okhla Industrial Area, Phase-II, New Delhi-110020
Tel.: 41603490
E-mail: info@haranandbooks.com/haranand@rediffmail.com
Shop online at: www.haranandbooks.com

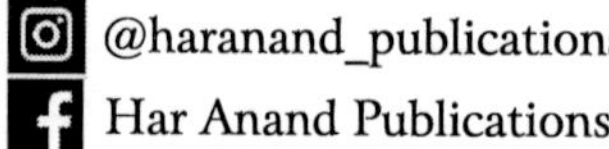

Reprint, 2024

Published by Ashok Gosain and Ashish Gosain for
Har-Anand Publications Pvt Ltd

Printed in India

Dedicated to
my wife, Professor Savitri Chandra "Shobha"
who left us on 27 February 2007.
She was always a source of succour and support.

Acknowledgements

1. Sri Rebala Lakshminarasa Reddy, Endowment Lecture, Sri Venkateswara University, Tirupati, 1976.
2. Presidential Address, Rajasthan History Congress, Ajmer, 1975.
3. *Occasional Paper Series*: 8, Urban History Association of India, 1986.
4. Paper read at Seminar on "Problems of Social and Economic History," Aligarh, Dec. 1968.
5. Report to UNESCO on project "Studies in Development," June 1983, also to Seminar on Heritage and Modern Challenges in the Arab World, Cairo, September 1984. The post-1947 section has been curtailed.
6. Paper presented at Symposium on "Russia, India and Central Asia: Historical Roots of Friendship and Cooperation," Tashkent, October 1986.
7. Paper presented to Indian Association for Asian and Pacific Studies, Kolkata, March 2002, printed *Journal of Indian Ocean Studies*, Vol.10 (1), Apr. 2002, pp.54-63.
8. Lecture, Staff College, J.N.U., 1983.
9. Lecture to mark the 211th Birth Anniversary of the Raja Ram Mohan Roy, Calcutta, May 1983.
10. Printed *India Today*, 1957.
11. Based on 93rd Nehru Anniversary Lecture, Nehru Memorial Museum and Library, November 1983.

12. Paper presented at Symposium on Secularism and National Unity, 1986.

13. Paper presented to Centre for Research in Rural Industrial Development, Chandigarh, Sept. 2001, printed in Haksar Memorial Vol.II, *Contributions in Remembrance*, ed. S. Banerjee, CRRID, Chandigarh, 2004, pp. 65-70.

Introduction

At the outset, let me pose the question: why do historians write history? The purpose or use of historical writing has varied from age to age and from region to region. The Greek historians glorified and upheld the institutions (including slavery) in the Greek city states, ascribing different virtues to them, e.g., stoicism as in Sparta or love of democracy as in Athens etc. The ancient Indian concept, as gleaned from the great epics, the Ramayana and the Mahabharata, was predominantly moral—of the victory of good over evil, of the upholding of the path of righteousness (*dharma*), and of the fulfillment of duty by all, unmindful of the consequences or hope of reward. Kings, warriors, men and women were, therefore, the instruments of a higher destiny. Simultaneously, there was the tradition of small states whose object was material gain, with the power resting on a ruler who was guided not so much by the Dharmashastras, as by considerations of polity (*rajniti*). These two traditions ran side by side, and shaped both conduct and legend writing (*itihas*).

Neither the Christian nor the Arab view of the purpose of history was strikingly different from the Hindu traditional views. However, the Church held pride of place in the Christian view of history since the Church alone was competent to guide the people in matters of morality or sin, or prepare men for entry into the Kingdom of Heaven. The Arab writing of history was aimed at glorifying Islam and those who laid down their lives for its advancement. The spiritual and the secular conquests went hand in hand. This may explain the dual character of much of Arab and subsequent history writing: the glorification of

Islam was meant to impress the common man and further firm up his belief. But the empire, which was even more crucial, depended on the ruling classes, the Sultan, his ministers, advisers, administrators, etc. The maintenance and further expansion of the Islamic empire thus became both a proof of the power of Islam (*ghalba-i-Islam*) and the means of sustaining the faith. This also implied firmly putting down all heterodox movements which might create a schism in the community, and hence weaken the empire.

History, therefore, had to be used to proclaim the glory of Islam, strengthen the empire or the states which succeeded, and sternly put down all heterodox movements. These are fully reflected in the writings of the 14th century Indian historian, Ziauddin Barani. Barani not only calls history the twin brother of the science of *hadis*. "It is also the province of history to relate the circumstances of the age of the Prophet and his companions and to explain and analyze that which strengthens the heart and confidence of both ancient and modern members of the Muslim community." Since Barani says there is no written proof of historical tradition, readers can only trust the historian himself, and that only if he was an orthodox Muslim. Of course, Barani considered that history taught by example and would benefit the Sultans, wazirs and nobles, but not "the evil, the base, the low-born," who had no use for history.

What about the more secular view which, as we have argued here was reflected in the *Arthashastra*?" It would be wrong to think that such a view made its appearance only with the introduction of western historiography by the British in the 19th century. By the time Abul Fazl wrote his books, the *Akbar Nama* and the *Ain-i-Akbari*, the central problem was no longer to what precise extent Islamic laws, customs, traditions could or could not be followed in India, but the manner in which the prosperity of the realm could be increased, and its foundations strengthened. And the lesson he drew was that it implied the ruler making no distinction between votaries of different religions, and seeking the active support and co-operation of all sections, especially all sections of the ruling elites—Rajputs, Afghans and Mughals—in the task of administration.

That history writing no longer reflected or could be used by narrow orthodox or racial groups was reflected in two developments during the 17th century in India: first, the appearance of history books written by Hindus (Ishwardas, Bhimsen, Mehta Nainsi's *Khyat* and *Vigat*, etc.), and, second, the discontinuation of official history writing by Aurangzeb. The latter step was perhaps more than a measure of economy. It reflected Aurangzeb's inability to mould history (as also poetry) writing for his own orthodox purposes, and hence to discourage it as far as possible.

The tradition of nationalist history writing in India and its use of history is well known. It was aimed at creating a sense of pride in India's past in order to compensate the low esteem in which the country and its culture was held by the colonial rulers (as distinct from the rare breed of people called the Indologists). Simultaneously, it tried to justify India's claim for freedom by arguing that the wherewithals of the qualities or institutions considered desirable, e.g. democracy, individualism, national unity had existed in the country before the arrival of the British, and any weakening was in large measure due to the influence of Colonialism.

This uncritical and somewhat romantic view of history had obviously to yield once India became free. But the change has been accompanied by a sea-change in the attitude to history in the west. The 19th century view of history was, basically, to justify and rationalize the European domination of the world, (i) by emphasizing certain intrinsic superior qualities of the west, e.g., rationalism, individualism, spirit of enterprise, humanism or secularism, etc., and (ii) to emphasize the lack of these superior qualities in the black, brown or yellow races, or the peoples inhabiting the Afro-Asian land mass. With decolonization following the second World War, and the growth of new centers of power outside Europe, the 19th century view of history could no longer be maintained.

How is world history being used today and to what use history is sought to be utilized in history? We cannot try to carry out a review of western history writing in the limited scope here, except to say that by far and large, the Eurocentric view of history has not really been abandoned, despite a definite trend of studying other non-European civilizations in a more sympathetic manner. Also, in place of empires, peoples, their lives and thought, behaviour, etc., are being given greater importance.

In the above context, to what use is history being used, or sought to be used in India? Governments desire, and it is possible to sympathize with their point of view, that history should teach love for the country, respect for the various people who made India their home, and their contribution to the fabric of Indian civilization. At a second move, government has also desired that the unity and stability of India, democratic values, secularism and a rational temper, and national integration should also be upheld by the historian. Since all these are closely related to the imperative need of India forging ahead as a united polity, the ideas of government would be shared by many historians. The question is, how to uphold these ideas without doing violence to or distorting history?

As is well known, every age puts its own questions to the past. Hence, the past has to be constantly re-interpreted. Such a process is always attended by pitfalls and controversy. The specific questions which the historian in India raises today are related to India's unity and development, as also its place in world comity, i.e., its contribution to the growth of human civilization, and the factors responsible for phases of stagnation and growth. This had made it necessary to determine the phases of development of Indian society, and the aspects of growth or lack of it in each phase. The question immediately arises whether India passed through the same phases of slavery and feudalism as Europe did up to the 15th century and whether it had any potentialities of developing a capitalist system independently? Also, the precise extent to which colonial rule aided or retarded such a development? While these questions are still very much in the realm of controversy, it has led to a more intensive study of social structures and developments in different parts of the world. To that extent, the intense phase of emphasizing the "uniqueness" of India, and hence eschewing any comparative studies is passing. But it does not mean that the historian is able to answer all the questions he himself raises. That is what makes history an un-ending quest.

The problems of development has also given a new dimension to Indian historical studies. With the rise of linguistic states, each state or linguistic cultural area is seeking the roots of its cultural identity. Thus, there has been a renewed interest in the growth of regional studies. The question has also been raised, within regions and between regions, why certain regions/areas, sections/communities develop/adapt more rapidly to the needs of modern society and technology than others? These are questions which can only be answered on the basis of detailed socio-cultural, economic, and a whole host of related factors.

These essays written over a period of a quarter century or more, reflect some of the above concerns. An attempt has been made in these essays to shift the emphasis from political history to change and development, and the extent to which traditional concepts have shaped developments in history and in free India. In this context, attention has been given to India's relations with Central Asia, and the "new great game" in the region. The role of education, and the urgent need to fight against fundamentalism, and to uphold values of secularism and rationalism have also been highlighted.

Many of these articles represent loud thinking rather than finished pieces of research. Also, since these essays were written or presented during the last twenty-five years, certain over-lap is inevitable for which, I hope, the readers would bear with me.

At the end, I am grateful to Shri Narendra Kumar, Chairman, Har-Anand Publications, and a valued friend, for insisting that I come out of my depression following the demise of my wife early this year, and search for unpublished articles tucked away in my files. I have done so, and hope that they will see the light of day so that I could happily, take leave from this phenomenal world.

I am also grateful to Annamma Abraham and Poonam Rawat of the Society for Indian Ocean Studies for typing the often decayed and brittle pages, and corrections.

Contents

CHAPTER I

Social Chang in Medieval India

I think one of the functions of an academic is to pose problems, even though he may not be able to answer them himself. One of the problems which I, along with many other people in the field of history, economics, political science, sociology, and now increasingly in the field of humanities, philosophy and even literature, are concerned with is the issue of social change. So, the main theme which I intend to put before you in these two lectures is the problem of social change, with particular reference to Medieval India.

At the outset, let me say that today the problem of social change is engaging the attention of increasingly larger numbers of people—not merely those in the academic field but also others in administration or broadly in the field of development. This concerns not merely people living in what are called the developing countries: in a manner of speaking, all countries in the world are developing, and this kind of dichotomy between developed and developing countries is only partially correct. The problem of social change is the concern not merely of the people in what are called the third world countries, or those which were formerly colonies of the developed countries. It is equally the concern of the developed countries, the capitalist as well as socialist, though, of course, the attitudes and specific problems of the two may differ. As far as the developing countries are concerned, one of the long range objectives in their development is to ensure for them a position of equality in he comity of nations and, at the same time, to help creating a society predicated on and perceived to be based on justice. Various terms—an egalitarian society or a socialist society or Hind Swaraj or socialism based on various religious tenets, Islam, Christianity, etc., are predicated to convey the concept of a society fundamentally based on justice, that is, where the disparities between different sections of society are minimized, and where the relationship between different sections of society is not based on exploitation.[1] As far as the Western countries are concerned, their present concerns, in particular, appear to be two-fold. There was, to a certain extent, what might be called a sense of guilt, a feeling that they had been responsible in the past for not having allowed these countries to develop. This sense of guilt was perhaps strongest after the Second World War. However, the feeling of guilt has been largely dissipated, a fact which is clear from the type of attitude which the Third World countries are encountering in the round of discussions with the Western countries regarding the problems of what is called "the new economic order." Apart from this, or their desire of helping the development of the former colonial countries, there is also, at the back of their mind, a wish to control and direct the development of the Third World countries in such a manner that the interests of the developed countries are safeguarded.

Therefore, when we study the problems of development, we must be extremely careful about the objectives of those who put forward various theories and concepts of development. In other words, their concepts of development and social change are not, what might be called, "value-free." They are often value loaded. In fact, I would say, where human affairs are concerned, there is nothing which is completely value free. Concepts have to be examined in the context of the particular

[1]For Gandhiji's ideas on a society based on justice, equality and service, see M. K. Gandhi: *Socialism of My Conception* (ed.) A. T. Hingorani, Bharatiya Vidya Bhawan.

situation in which they were put forward. Also, the structure of the society to which a person belonged, his background, motivations, etc., cannot be considered irrelevant to the enquiry.

Thus, before the Second World War, there was a deep-seated belief of oriental societies being unchanging. The "unchanging orient' was a terms which was so widely used that it was hardly questioned. But the "unchanging orient" is changing rapidly and has changed. Obviously, it does not mean that this change is sudden and that the oriental societies were incapable of change earlier, i.e., before the Second World War. One can only say that the processes of change have accelerated. But these processes have accelerated in the West, as in the rest of the world. The point is recent developments have undermined the earlier belief that processes of change did not affect the Orient. In fact, one may argue that the earlier belief was based on the perception and interests of the colonial powers. The colonial powers were aware that they might be accused of hindering the development of their colonies. In speaking of an "unchanging orient" they transferred, so to say, lack of development to inscrutable factors beyond their control. Thus, they obscured the fact that the oriental society of their imagination was one which they themselves had helped to fashion. The processes of colonialism had meant retarded development. Instead of admitting this before the rest of the world, the historians who basically represent colonial interests postulated an Orient, which was "incapable" of change. The interesting point is that this picture of an orient which was unchanging, and impervious to the processes of change put forward by Western scholars found ready acceptance among large numbers of intellectuals from these countries.

It is a well- known adage that the true test of slavery is that you not merely enslave a person but convince him that his enslavement is logical and necessary.[2] Thus, the idea that western rule or colonialism was necessary to shake these countries out of their slumber or to effect at least a minimum of change in societies which had been static for long periods was sought to be rooted deeply. I do not want in this context to recall the words of Macaulay, because he is recalled too often and not always justly. Many of the things Macaulay did or said were hardly original. He merely echoed many of the prejudice about India and the orient which were then current in the West. For Macaulay, the entire oriental civilization could be shut up in an almirah. This was an index of his ignorance and prejudice and that of the class he represented. Hence, we need not talk about it further. But let me recall the words of Sir Charles Eliot whose work *History of India as told by its own Historians* continued by Dowson has been used by several generations of historians. In his Introduction, Eliot put forward a philosophy and an understanding of oriental society. He contrasted the Oriental society with the Greek society and said that in Oriental societies one does not find "the vicissitudes of institutions, social, political and religious." As far as Eliot was concerned, Oriental history was nothing but "the monotony of successive conspiracies, revolts, intrigues, murders and fratricides and the rise and fall of dynasties."[3] However, India is rich in institutional, social, economic and religious development for which rich material is to be found. The new emphasis on the study of the *Dharmasastras* and the corpus of works on *Rajaniti* in Sanskrit and other languages has made this apparent. These, in fact, help in determining the stages in the development of society in India. There is a well-known adage among historians that you will find the type of source material which

[2]Arnold, *Lectures on Modern History,* as quoted by C. Eliot, *The History of India etc.,* 1st ed. London, 1867, reprinted Kitab Mahal, Allahabad, Vol., 1969, p. XX.

[3]Eliot, Vol. I., p. XIX.

you are looking for. Time and again I have had the opportunity of assigning to my research students a problem for which apparently there were no sources available. But once the student started looking at the source material from that particular point of view, he· found that not only was the information on the topic available, sometimes it was so rich that it was impossible for it to be encompassed in a single thesis.

There has been an old controversy whether the Indians had any history at all. I do not want to enter into this controversy. Obviously, those who were arguing that the Indians did not have a history meant by it the enunciation of the doings of the great which was regarded as history till the Second World War. They also argued that the Indians did not have a sense of history or that if there was a concept of history in the Orient, it was repetitive. I would like to contest this belief which is still widespread. Unlike the thinking in many of the western countries, if we take a deep look at the Indian tradition, it certainly does not reflect a society which was static or unchanging. We are familiar with the Indian concept of the *Yugas,* the *Satyuga, Dwapar, Treta* and *Kali.* This evolutionary concept has not been adequately appreciated. The features of society during various stages as they have been enunciated may not be acceptable to us. But the basic philosophy is of evolution of society, the idea that society changes from one age to another, and also when the basic structure of society changes, everything else—the code of morality (*dharma*), social institutions, code of behaviour etc. all change. This is summated in the word *Yugadharma.* This concept of change may be compared to the western, or rather the Hegelian concept of change as a continuous, upward movement, whereas the Indian concept was its opposite— it was one of continuous decline leading to an apocalypse *(pralaya)* after which the cosmos *(srishti)* would be recreated, and the same cycle would be repeated. Now outwardly, evolution was cyclical in nature. But the movement from birth *(srishti)* to *pralaya* was in terms of cosmic time, not in terms of human time. Therefore, if we carefully analyze the concept of *yugadharma* which was widely accepted, we shall see that it implied a belief in continuous change, of continuous flux of institutions, morality and behaviour, philosophical beliefs and structure of society. Thus, change was all pervading.

The concept of continuous decline in moral standards leading to an age of decadence *(kali-yuga)* perhaps led to an attitude of looking upon change with suspicion and of projecting a "golden age" in the past—an attitude which is replicated in many religions, including Christianity. However, these lost, idyllic kingdoms could be restored, if the right leader in the shape of a Prophet or a God incarnate should appear, and be recognized. Hence the change desired for was always projected in the shape of a "restoration." These are psychological attitudes which, perhaps, persist in our country even today. Also, religious ideas and movements have a special importance in the context of social change and merit close study and attention. For this, a pre-requisite is the availability of critical texts of works dealing with these aspects.

The process of change can never be even or constant. There have been phases in our history where the process of change seems to have been virtually congealed. But there were also phases when the process of change was fairly rapid. For a country with 5000 years of history, this flux cannot be regarded as unusual. Also, why should we believe that the pace of change, or the factor of time in the process of change in the world as a whole, should more or less correspond to the time factor in the process of change in the West? The Greek society or the Greco-Roman society, which is considered to be the classical age in Europe, disintegrated around the fifth century and was followed by an "age of darkness" or the feudal age. Each of these cycles lasted about a thousand years. In other parts of the world also, people have passed through a number of stages. Thus, in India we can talk of phases: of a tribal society giving way to a society in which village communities co-existed with a fairly centralized state structure (the Nanda-Maurya age) which in turn, gradually disintegrated and was replaced by a feudal society. The main features of these societies, their inner contradictions, processes of change etc., are all a subject of controversy among historians. It would be futile to try to find in Indian social development all the stages of development and their specific features as found in European societies. In fact, it would be necessary to identify the specific features of Indian society. I would like to be wary of the claim of Indian society being "unique." For the historian, every society is unique, just as every individual human being is unique. Nor does denial of uniqueness mean that the developments in India and Europe were basically similar. These are some of the well-known pitfalls of undertaking a comparative study between vastly dissimilar civilizations.

The unique features in India may be considered caste and the village community. A great deal has been written on caste. I do not intend to try to enter into the details of the dynamics of caste in India. An assumption which was strengthened by the writings of Max Weber was that caste was the biggest inhibiting factor in the process of change in Indian society. Of course, a number of other ideas were also put forward in an explicit or an implicit manner to establish the same point, viz., the Indian belief in "fatalism," effect of climate etc.[4] Students of medieval India would be familiar with the idea that Indians lost against the Turks because the latter came

[4]For a recent discussion, see Morris D. Morris, etc., "Towards a Reinterpretation of Nineteenth Century Indian History," *The Indian Social and Economic History Review*, New Delhi, Vol. V, No. 1, 1968, pp. 1-108.

from colder climates and as such were supposed to be more hardy. This subtly propagated the belief that it was not possible for people living in the warmer climates to fight successfully against people coming from colder climates! Even the great historian, Sir Jadunath Sarkar, who was a pioneer in the field of research and one of the tallest amongst medieval Indian historians, could not rise above this concept. He considered that a major factor in the downfall of the Mughal Empire was the "stoppage of the flow of the right type of immigrants" from Bukhara, Samarqand, Iran and Arabia, i.e., the colder climes. "When this flow stopped, the Empire shriveled up like a tree cut off from its sap."[5] It can be perceived easily that this idea had little to do with medieval history. It was really an argument put forward by the British Imperialist historians to establish the superiority of the British over the Indians, Asians and Africans. The Indians had to be convinced that just as they were not able to gain a victory against the Turks who came from a colder climate, they could not hope to gain a victory against the British who like the Turks, came from a colder climate. Thus, geography had fated that the Indians be ruled by people coming from colder climates! This "vivifying stream of immigrants" coming from Iran, Turan etc., was nothing but the British products of Cambridge and Oxford who were sent to rule over India as I.C.S., I.P.S. etc., without whom India could not hold together.

These concepts now appear to us to be puerile. But during British rule, the concept of racial superiority, which found its ultimate form in Hitlerite Germany, was fairly widespread and tacitly accepted by the European powers. In fact, even today the concept of racial superiority has not been given up. There are many people, particularly in South Africa and including some scientists, who would like to prove that there

[5]Jadunath Sarkar, in *Later Mughals,* Orient Books, reprinted, Delhi, 1971, II, p. 308.

is something inherently superior in the blood of the white people. Or, that European science, European values etc., are innately superior.[6] The influence of these ideas on history writing could be a separate subject of study.

The theory of the inherent superiority of the men from colder climates was so crude that it could. not have been continued for long. The surprising thing is that it continued to figure in our historical writings for such a long period. In fact, it figures in some of our school and college text books even today. In scholarly circles, this theory had been discarded long ago in favour of the theories associated with Max Weber. According to Max Weber, oriental society was so hierarchical and rigid that it was incapable of adjusting itself to the needs of an industrial society where mobility is considered to be the essence. He contrasted the Oriental societies, which were hierarchical in structure, and were rigid and hidebound, and based on tradition and custom, with the Western societies which were not as hierarchical. Max Weber highlighted the elements of mobility, both vertical and horizontal, in these societies so that people coming from the lower sections of society, whether they were artisans or engineers could climb into the ruling class, and where people possessing specialized knowledge could move from one branch of the economy to the other without losing their hierarchical or ritual status or standing in society.[7]

Max Weber's ideas continued to hold sway in scholarly circles till the end of World War II or the beginning of the decolonizing period. Caste is no longer considered a major inhibiting factor in economic development as shown by the

[6]For a further discussion, see present author's article, "A Note on the Decentring of History and Apprehension by All People of their History," *Diogenes,* UNESCO, Spring 1972, No. 77, pp. 92-109, also author's *Essays on Medieval Indian History*, O.U.P., 2003, pp. 505-522.

[7]This is found interspersed in Max Weber's Writings. See for instance his *The Sociology of Religion,* Methuen, London, 1965, p. 41.

four Five Year Plans. In fact, caste has emerged as a pressure group which demands more money for the social, economic and educational development of its members. It is somewhat surprising that most of our scholars, whether they were in the field of literature or sociology or history, had, till now, largely ignored the evidence in historical and literary writings that caste was not really an inhibiting factor in choosing professions; and that people drawn from different castes had occupied the position of rulers at various times in history, or were closely associated with the ruler. This refers to the celebrated controversy regarding the origin of the Rajputs,[8] or the mixed caste origin of the Kayasthas. Even as far as trade and commerce is concerned, the people who engaged themselves in trade and commerce were drawn from vastly varying caste backgrounds. There has been considerable mobility in handicrafts and industry also. However, when practical experience demonstrated that caste was not as rigid as some scholars had imagined it to be, many scholars started going back to the sources and found that there had been a much greater element of mobility between *varnas* in ancient as well as medieval times than had been imagined before. That there had been considerable mobility between the *varnas* in the ancient period was accepted. However, it was believed that castes became rigid in the period following the death of Harsha. The large numbers of castes and sub-castes which are mentioned in the sources at the time can be considered an indication of growing subdivision and rigidity. This theory has been challenged by some recent historians. Thus, Professor R.S. Sharma thinks that many of the sub-castes represented tribal people who were being continuously absorbed into Hinduism. Decline of trade and commerce and

[8]For a recent survey, see B.D. Chattopadhyaya, "Origin of the Rajputs: The Political, Economic and Social Processes in Early Medieval Rajasthan," *Indian Historical Review,* Vikas Publishing House, New Delhi, Vol. III, No.1, July, 1976, pp. 59-82.

the growth of localism following the growth of feudalism were other factors responsible for the proliferation of sub-castes *(jati)*. The growth of sub-castes *(jatis),* he argues was a result of the growth of Hindu society paralleled, later on, by economic decline and political disintegration.[9] Thus, lack of economic and social development in a particular period or a slow process of development, must be considered the sum total of many complex intertwining factors. It cannot be explained by one factor alone, much less by false notions regarding the working of caste, or effect of climate, or fatalism or belief in fate.

This brings me to our understanding of the so called "medieval period." The thinking of many of our historians has been patterned very largely on the thinking of European historians. During the 18th century, European historians divided their society into the classical age, followed by the age of darkness or the medieval period which gave way to the Renaissance or the age of reason and enlightenment. From this followed the three-fold division of society into ancient, medieval and modern. When Indian historians started the process of conceptualizing Indian society, they took this model and tried to fit it on Indian society. Sometimes, Marxists are accused of trying to fit the Marxist structure of society on situations which are very different. It seems that this is what, in a manner of speaking, the traditional modern historians have been doing for a long time. First, they tried to look for a

[9]See R.S. Sharma, *Social Changes in Early Medieval India* (C. A.D. 500-1200) Delhi, 1969. c/f the remark of John Wilson in *Indian Caste* (Poona, 1877; reprinted Deep Publications, New Delhi, 1976, p. 54).

"The Mixed Castes," must have originated principally from the increase of occupations in the Hindu community, brought about by the growing demands and division of labour, and by the circumstance of the dominant people (the Aryas, to be immediately noticed), coming in contact with aboriginal tribes, which keeping in the main beyond the pale of Hinduism, have either been ultimately degraded, or have maintained for themselves in their own retreats a precarious independence."

classical age in India. After some time, it was decided that the only period in Indian history which merits this description is the period of Gupta rule. And so, Gupta rule began to be described as a Golden Age or the classical age, as is the title given to it in the Vidya Bhawan series covering this period. It is not *a* classical age, but *the* classical age. That is, there could not be a classical age either before or after this, or anywhere else in the country as in the case of Europe where there was only one classical age, viz., the Greko-Roman age. In Europe, the classical age was followed by an age of darkness in which there was little economic and scientific growth and society became rigid. So, in India the period of "Muslim Rule" was chosen as being virtually the age of darkness. But then there must be a renaissance. So Rammohan Roy was found to be the originator of the renaissance. What had happened in India before Rammohan, whether we had at any time lost our link with classical learning as the Europeans had done, and whether it was correct to call it a rebirth as Renaissance literally means, whether in India the so-called Renaissance was accompanied by far-reaching economic and social changes, and of scientific discoveries as in the west which led to far reaching changes in social values and outlook are questions which were not posed.

My main point is that our historians have been guided by the Western European models for far too long. The Marxist model can act as a corrective, but, in turn, should not be allowed to become a rigid frame work. This is not the place to raise the problem of stratification in Indian society. Regarding the classical age, (I would like to avoid the concept of a Golden Age which is unhistorical), if by that is meant an age in which certain standards were set and these standards became the basis on which subsequent generations were guided, then in India which is a sub-continent, we have not one but a series of classical ages. After all, the Gupta Empire extended only to Northern India. Does it mean that the South was incapable of evolving a classical age? As far as Southern India is concerned, the Chola Age was in no way inferior in terms of peace over a large tract of land, economic expansion, cultural development and artistic creativity as compared to the Gupta period in the North. And what about the Mughal period? Today, we are proud of the architecture created by the Mughals, and of the Mughal miniatures—especially now that they are being avidly sought after by tourists. (Unfortunately, we only start praising something after the Europeans discover it. Even our classical music, particularly the sitar, has been rediscovered by the younger generation *via* the Hippies). Anyhow, in terms of setting the standard whether it was in the field of architecture, or music, or literature, or food; or whether it was the manners or forms of address in polite society, the Mughal age can certainly qualify to be called a classical age. However, from my point of view, if we give up this futile exercise of looking for the classical age or ages, and stop being exercised whether India had a renaissance or not, and instead start a sustained study of the concrete processes of change, its agents and consequences, its inter connections, we shall have a better understanding of the historical process in our country. For the purpose, it is necessary not only to restudy historical sources, particularly historical records which we have in abundance and which we have only scratched so far, but also make a study of literature. A study of literary sources is important for values, outlook and the perception of change. Perception of a new order of things or change in our outlook is perhaps grasped more readily by a great writer than by an historian. The understanding of history throughout the early medieval and the late medieval period starting from the time of *Rajatarangini* is that history is the doings of the rulers and their immediate advisers. In this scheme of things, the common people largely did not figure. Their trials and tribulations, their sentiments and outlook can be gleaned, to some extent, by a study of the writings of the period. Again, literature itself has a vast variety. We have, the ballad form which is sometimes called epic poetry, dealing with the lives of heroes. We have the erotic *(sringara)* poetry which has been called court poetry. Then we have the writings of the saint-poets the Adyars, the Alwars in the South and the Bhakti and sufi saints in the North. These, within their limitations, did reflect popular and lower class sentiments. Other types of hagiological literature may be added to this. The popular leaders associated with the various religious movements were not an integral part of the ruling classes, although it was often not possible for them to dis-associate themselves completely with them. The manner in which they perceived the social reality, the values and attitude of the ruling class, as well as the sentiments and aspirations of the common people, again, provides us a vantage or a useful point of observation.

In discussing the problems of change, we must be careful what exactly we mean by change. There has been a good deal of discussion amongst sociologists, social anthropologists, historians and economists on the problem of change in society. Of course I would not exclude philosophers, for philosophers are also very much concerned with the problem of change. Broadly speaking, the processes, of change can be divided into two broad categories; structural change, where the movement— whether it is a movement of protest or something more than that, is in one way or another aims at or leads up to, effecting structural changes. The second type of change, where structural changes are not involved, has been called developmental[10] or positional. Although we may distinguish structural and developmental changes for

[10]Henry A. Landsberger (ed.), *Rural Protest: Peasant Movements and Social Change,* 1974, Introduction.

purposes of study, they are not necessarily unconnected with each other. Here, the perception of Marx is important. Marx distinguishes between technological change or change in the modes of production which comprises methods and relationship of production. Then there are changes in what he calls the superstructure—the legal, political, intellectual processes which interact with changes in the methods and relations of production. Change in the mode of production is continuous and has a bearing on society as a whole. We are today passing through extraordinarily rapid changes in technology, i.e., the methods of production leading to changes in other branches of life. Changes in the structure although they are not co-related to structural changes, do have an important bearing on structure itself.

For a meaningful study of change in Indian society, a careful study of the specificities of Indian society is necessary. I have already mentioned one of these—caste. Another specificity of Indian society is the village community. A good deal of literature has grown around the problem of the village community. The early British administrators were struck with it, and a considerable body of literature on the subject grew up during the 18th and 19th centuries. These writings had a considerable impact. In one sense, the national movement itself was inclined to attach great importance to the institution of the village community, largely because some of the western thinkers had called them "petty village republics." This was considered in some way a vindication of the claim that Indian society was neither hierarchical, nor autocratic but that it was deeply and fundamentally democratic. This strengthened the Indian claim for freedom. If the British left, the Indian people who had democratic urges and democratic institutions would be capable of maintaining and defending democracy. It was in this context that the "village republic" and "village community" received considerable encouragement and commendation from nationalist thinkers.[11]

However, the manner in which the village community was perceived by social scientists was very different. The historians were of the opinion that the village community provided a justification for autocracy, for the villager was so completely absorbed in his petty round of existence and caste-based responsibilities that he was not at all bothered as to what happened at the national level. Therefore any set of rulers could come and dominate the country, and as far as the peasant was concerned, as long as his rights were not tampered with and he was called upon to pay only the customary dues, he would accept readily whosoever may be the ruler at the centre. For the economist, the autarchic village community was the root cause of the rigid, unchanging character of Indian society. As long as the village was self-sufficient economically, a national market could hardly develop. "Economic development" was, therefore, confined largely to the towns and since the towns were few in number, there was insufficient potential for development. Even Marx, who was concerned above all with social change, considered the village community to be the fundamental basis for the unchanging character of Indian society, in fact, for the unchanging character of oriental society as a whole. He said that British rule was the only force which carried out a far reaching social revolution in India because by their economic and administrative policies, the British undermined the village community.[12] Thus, the village community has been a central feature in the thinking about the processes of change in Indian society.

[11]See B.R. Grover, "The Concept of the Village Community in North India during the Mughal Age and the Pre-British Era," (Paper read at Indian Institute of Advanced Study, Simla, 1966, mimeographed).

[12]Karl Marx, *The British Rule in India,* New York, *Herald Tribune,* 10 June 1853; *Capital,* Vol. I, Ch. XIV, Sec. 4.

The postulates on the basis of which Indian society was, at one time, considered rigid and unchanging, merit a close examination. In particular, the phases of historical development, that is, the European model of a classical society followed by an age of darkness, giving place to a renaissance has to be jettisoned. The specific features of Indian society, in particular caste and the village community need careful study in the context of change, i.e., not in isolated form, but in the context of the development of society as a whole.

II

In studying the processes of growth, the study of the peasants and peasant society has great importance. Sociologists, that is, western sociologists have, so to say, "rediscovered" the peasant. Till now, sociologists in the west were mainly concerned with the urban worker and the other segments of city population. To an Indian, to talk of the "rediscovery" of the peasant sounds strange because in our literature and in the thinking of many of our leaders pride of place has been given to the peasants. It is not merely Gandhiji who attached so much importance to the peasant. Village and village life are considered to be the basis of the Indian culture and form a running thread in our literature and in our thinking. Of course, one may dispute the extent to which rural values are emphasized by individual writers during specific periods. Generally, Indian writers did not idealize the peasant, but they did attach special importance to rural life. At the same time, a villager (*gunwar*) was considered uncultured, and a citizen *(nagarik)* cultured and sophisticated. But what exactly is a peasant? Does he have some universal values, or is he in the product of a specific socioeconomic system or of a definite cultural milieu? As an historian, I am suspicious of "universalist" definitions. For instance, Barrington More and Wolf, in a study of the peasants came to the conclusion that the most characteristic feature of a peasant is that he has "low status." The authors go on to say that "the typical feature of a peasant is subordination to a landed upper class, sharp cultural distinction and a considerable degree of de facto possession of land." The definition has been put forward in such a manner that it could apply to a peasant living in what may be called a feudal society as well as to a peasant living in a capitalist society. According to this definition, social structures affect the peasant's way of life only marginally. Wolf says that the peasants are primarily rural cultivators, who "make autonomous decisions regarding the process of cultivation" (unlike the worker who has to conform to a decision by the owner or the merchant) and whose surpluses are transferred to a dominant group of rulers."[13] Now, the "dominant group of rulers" could be tribal chiefs, feudal lords, capitalist owners or a state in which surplus is extracted from the peasant either for personal consumption or for the development of society as a whole. Such a definition is not helpful to the historians interested in the processes of social change.

The stages of the development of village society which had a considerable influence on society as a whole can be divided into a number of phases. The earliest phase may be called the phase of the breakdown of tribalism and the establishment of village communities. There have been different processes in the transformation of tribals into peasants in different parts of the world. As far as India is concerned, the transformation of the tribal into peasant is more or less synonymous with the establishment of what we call the village community, which, in turn, is linked to the emergence of the caste system. There

[13]Barrington Moore and Wolfe in *Rural Protest,* loc. cit., pp. 50-75 c/f R H. Hilton, *The English Peasantry in the Later Middle Ages,* O.U.P., 1975, pp.8-13.

are different theories about the emergence of the caste system into which I need not enter here. According to K.M. Panikkar, the caste system enabled different tribes, whether they are Aryan or non-Aryan, to be welded into a common polity.[14] Thus, the process of transformation of tribals into a peasant society based on village communities was accompanied by far-reaching cultural changes: in religion, the old Vedic gods, many of whom reflected a tribal were gradually replaced by universal gods, Shiva and Vishnu. Buddhism rose at about the same time. The rise of Buddhism which was a universalist religion *par excellence,* was, thus, a part of the process of social change outlined above.[15] The process was a complex and long drawn out. The large scale use of the iron technology, and the rise of large empires in the eastern region of India where this technology was developed, falls in this historical period. It is the duty of modern historian to analyze these various facets and see how one influenced the other. It is interesting to note that this phase began roughly with the great *Mahabharata* war which may be regarded the last great war amongst the tribes. Not only the leading Aryan tribes, the Kauravas and its off-shoot, the Pandavas, but many other tribes including non-Aryan tribes and petty kingships were drawn into this battle. It is significant that according to the Indian tradition, the *Mahabharata* war coincides with the beginning of a new age, the "Kali Age." In other words, it was the perception of the writers, philosophers etc., that a new phase of society or a new phase of culture or a new *yuga* with its own code of conduct *(dharma)* begins with the *Mahabharata* war. Unfortunately, in our text books, this phase up to the rise of Buddhism is

[14]K.M. Panikkar, *A Survey of Indian History,* Asia, First published 1947, reprinted, June, 1957, pp. 12-14.

[15]See for instance, D.D. Kosambi, *The Culture and Civilisation of Ancient India,* Vikas, reprinted, 1972, pp. 91-95.

vaguely called the Vedic Age, sometimes divided into Vedic and the later Vedic ages. Thus, not the elements of change but the elements of continuity are emphasized. The question of value judgement, of dubbing the Kaliyuga as "an age of decadence" in which true *dharma* could not be observed, is a question of, judgement or belief. In the universities, every succeeding generation of students thinks that things had worsened and were much better in their times. Perhaps there is a human tendency to imagine that things do not improve but worsen. As far as the modern historians are concerned, a new interpretation is being given to the *Mahabharata* war, linking it with the beginning of the iron technology and the replacement of tribal territories with large empires.[16] Although a number of scholarly works have been produced, an integrated study of this crucial, formative age, integrating archaeological and literary evidence has yet to be carried out. The task of the modern historian is to study the various aspects of change in the field of technology, economy, social structure as well as in the spheres of ideology and culture. This is a difficult task and I would expect other social scientists, including philosophers, such as Prof. K.S. Murty, to play an active part in this enterprise. Change and continuity are constant features in history. It would be wrong to emphasize only one of these to the exclusion of the other.

The phase of tribal breakdown culminated in the establishment of the Mauryan Empire. The Mauryan Empire was the first truly universalits empire in the Indian context, embracing all India. It is significant that this universalist empire virtually accepted Buddhism as a state religion. Till then, Buddhism was more truly universalist in spirit than the Hindu religion. It would be seen that the rise of the caste system as we know it, and the formation of the village

[16]See N.R. Bannerji, *The Iron Age in India,* Delhi, 1965; *Mahabharata: Myth and Reality,* (eds.) S.P. Gupta, K.S. Ramachandran, Agam Prakashan, Delhi, 1976.

communities belong roughly to the same historical phase. A primary feature of the village community was the combination of agriculture with handicrafts. This, in turn, was based on distribution of labour on the basis of caste. Thus, caste and economic functionalism were combined.

There is a long standing debate amongst historians, sociologists and others whether the village community implied common ownership of land or common responsibility for the collection of land revenue, and whether it had common responsibility for the administration of the village life in general? The difficulty is, when we discuss village community it is sometimes, imagined that it is something static itself. Obviously, the village community must have evolved just as the rest of society evolved. My own guess is—I would not say that it is anything more than a guess because I have not made a special study of the sources of the ancient period of Indian history—that in the early phase, when the tribal communities were being transformed into village communities, there would have been a strong tradition of common ownership of land. One of the distinctive features of tribal societies is the strong tradition of land being held in common by the tribe as a whole, though of course, even within the tribes, the process of differentiation develops. So, in those areas where the tribal tradition was strong, the tradition of land being held in common by the village community would have been strong. If land was held in common, obviously, the responsibility of paying land revenue, of administering the affairs of the community would also have been largely in common. But as the village community develops, as private ownership of land grows, the common features also get eroded. By the time we come to the medieval period, there was hardly any tradition left of land being considered the common property of the village community. But a definite statement can be made only on the basis of detailed regional studies. Even today, there are large tribal belts in India with different traditions. At what phase land ownership became largely individual is another point which merits detailed study by historians. Karl Marx who was no specialist of Indian history, but whose perception of the forces by historical evolution in many countries is remarkable, was, at first, of the opinion that the lack of private property in land was the great "desideratum" of Asian civilizations. Therefore, he considered that a second specific feature of the village community was the common ownership of land.[17] But from the detailed studies of the 16th, 17th and 18th centuries which have now been conducted, innumerable references to land being private property are available. From the end of the 16th century, we have many sale deeds of land. Thus, theoretically, land was not common property. In practice, there were many difficulties, because the peasants were reluctant to land being sold to "outsiders." Thus, sometimes the permission of the village community or of the ruler was necessary for sale of land to an "outsider." In Maharashtra, all the village officials had to bear witness to a sale deed. Land was, perhaps, more freely saleable in towns or their immediate neighbourhood. Conditions restricting free sale of land may have varied form region to region, according to local traditions. There were strong vestiges of tribalism in some regions of India. In fact, the process of tribes giving way to village communities is a long drawn out process. It continued throughout our history and is at work even today.

To resume, although land was not generally held in common during the medieval period, the village community

[17]"The absence of Property in land is indeed the key to the whole of the East." Marx to Engels (Manchester) 6 June (1853), *Marx and Engels Correspondence,* National Book Agency, Calcutta, 1955.

But see also letter dated London 14 June, 1853, "In the broken hill country south of kishna, property in land and soil does seem to have existed."

did have a certain responsibility for the collective payment of land revenue. We have, in medieval literature, reference to a section of peasants who are called *khud-kashta*. I have made some study of this phenomenon with the help of Rajasthani and Marathi documents.[18] The *khud-kashta* are the same whom in the 18th century the British administrators designated "resident cultivators." This was the body of people who claimed to be the original settlers on land in the village. Sometimes they traced their origin to a common ancestor, real or imaginary, just as every tribe had a real or imagined common ancestor or a common totem with whom the tribe associated itself. Little attempt has been made to trace back the origin of these "resident cultivators." However, if we were to take an example from England, even during the 13th century, the division of village society into resident cultivators and "outsiders" was a familiar one.[19] In India, with strong tribal traditions, this concept may have been even older.

The "resident cultivators" or the *khud-kashta* undoubtedly constituted what modern sociologists call "the dominant castes." Even today, there are villages where land is held in the main by one caste, or by a combination of these. In Akbar's time, the castes of zamindars in various parganas have been given in the *Ain*. We do not know whether there was any concordance between the castes of the zamindars and of the *khud-kashta*. The *khud-kashta* were the owners of the land (*malik-i-zamin*) they cultivated, and had the right to bequeath their land, or alienate or mortgage it. In addition, they had two distinct responsibilities. One was the obligation to cultivate as much land as possible. To cultivate or not to

[18] Satish Chandra, "Some Aspects of Indian Village Society in Northern India during the 18th Century, The Position and Role of *Khud-kasht* and *Pahi-kashta*," *I.H.R.*, Vol. 1. No. I, pp.51-64, also in *Essays on Medieval Indian History*, O.U.P, 2003, pp.168-92.

[19] Hilton, *The English Peasantry*, loc. cit. "Outsiders were excluded from village affairs...," p.55.

cultivate was not the question of one's individual will, because the amount of land one cultivated had a direct bearing not only on the income of the state—the sinews on the basis of which armies marched, but also the basis on which cities expanded and trade grew. The entire city population, whether it was the artisans, the servants, the traders or the administrators, depended upon the foodgrains produced in the countryside. So the question of how much a peasant cultivated did not remain an individual decision; but became an obligation due to the State. There are many references in Mughal literature of local officials being asked to persuade the *khud-kashta* peasants to cultivate as much land as they could; if they were not willing to comply, to threaten them, and if they did not still yield, to punish them. Thus, cultivation was not merely a right, or a way of life; it was an obligation to the State and to the rest of the society.

The second responsibility which the *khud-kashta* had was of paying the land revenue collectively. Once the share of each individual *khud-kashta* peasant had been assessed, the entire body of the *khud-kashta* was held responsible for the payment of the land revenue due from the village as a whole. Thus, if any individual did not cultivate his field or for some reason left the village and went away, the responsibility of paying his share of the land revenue would fall on the rest of the *khud-kashta* community *(biradari)*. Thus, it is the *khud-kashta* who really constituted or were the core of the village community. It is they who formed the Panchayat. It is they who had the privilege of the pick up the best village lands. They had certain other privileges as well: they could use the produce of the jungles, or the village pond. They had also what in Maharashtra is called *man pan* i.e., certain social privileges. For instance, at the time of festivals, they had a privileged position. They were also exempted from some type of village ceases.

Apart from the *khud-kashta* peasants, there· was a second body of peasants who were considered basically outsiders.

The word used for the "outsider" varies from area to area. In the north-western part, it was *pahi,* in Maharashtra *upari.* In Rajasthan, the word used is *palti.* There must have been a separate word in southern India as well. The *pahis* were not owners of the land. But they could not be dispossessed as long as they paid the land revenue. As distinct from the *khud-kashta* who paid land revenue at a concessional rate, the *pahis* were required to pay land-revenue at a market rate, except in some special situations, such as the rehabilitation of a ruined village.

Who were these "outsiders" and where did they come from? An analysis of this would help us in tracing the evolution of the village community in India since the break up of the tribal settlements. To begin with, they might have been the slaves of the village community as a whole, or they might have been some kind of bonded labour. Kautilya speaks of *asita* lands, or lands brought under the plough with the help of slave labour. According to Kosambi,[20] as more and more land was brought under cultivation, and it was difficult to control and organize slave labour: the slaves had to be freed and the earlier forms were replaced by village communities. Thus, there was more than one way for the formation of village communities. Where a village community evolved out of a slave society, the number of land owing *(khud-kashta)* peasants may have been smaller, and the number of serf or semi-serf peasants larger. In such a situation internal mobility might have been greater with the semi-serf and scheduled caste peasant of one village becoming a *pahi* or a tenant cultivator in another. As late as the 18th century, Warren Hastings equated the *pahis* of Bengal to low-caste untouchables.

It is possible to view the village community either in the context of a relatively stable peasant population and a stable land-man ratio, or in the context of a slow but definite growth

[20]Kosambi, *The Culture and Civilisation,* loc. cit., pp. 148-52.

of population in which case there would be a growing pressure on land. Normally, such pressure would be relieved by bringing marginal land under cultivation, or by the settlement of new villages. Over-assessment or natural calamities sometimes forced *khud-kashta* peasants to become "vagrant riatts" (a term used by Warren Hastings)[21] i.e., *pahis*. Thus village society looked stable only from the outside. In practice, it was continually changing, due to internal and external forces, and trying to adapt itself to new circumstances. The basic structure did not change, but within the structure there were changes which were not inconsequential. The relationships of the *khud-kashta* with the zamindar, if there was one, and with the *pahis* were important factors. Sometimes, the zamindar brought in *pahis* from outside in order to beat down or overawe recalcitrant *khud-kashta* peasants. In course of time, these *pahis* could themselves hope to become *khudkashta*. There was no basic line of demarcation between a *kud-kashta* and a *pahi*, but their proportion in a particular village was an index of many internal pressures.

Thus, the evolution of the village community, and elements of stability and change in rural society in India are important facets of social change which merit careful study.

Let me call attention to another aspect of social change: caste mobility. When talking of mobility within the caste system, one should be clear not to confuse *varna* with *jati*. Unfortunately, the English word *caste* has created a great deal of confusion. The word *caste* is often used both for *varna* as well as *jati* (or popularly, *jat*). Broadly, *varna* is a category, or a station or *etat* in the medieval European sense.[*] While

[21] *Hastings Papers*, British Museum, Add. Ms 19090, quoted in *Khud-Kasht* and *Pahi-kasht*, loc cit.

[*] The four-fold division of Indian society may be compared to the medieval European concept of the three estates—priests, warrior and the rest. The four-fold division of society in India, itself evolved out of an earlier and similar categorization. The emergence of the traders (*Vaishyas*) as a distinct category perhaps indicated a greater degree of commercial-ization in Indian society as compared to medieval European society.

varna may be called a broad concept or a rationalization, *jati* which is based on a sense of hierarchy may be called a social reality. The story in the *Puranas* regarding the origin of the different *varnas* implies that the *jat* preceded *varnas*; and that there was need to give sanction to the *varna* theory by attributing to it a divine origin. To avoid confusion, we shall use the word "caste" here to denote *jati* only. The castes included in the various *varnas* could not quite coincide and varied from area to area. In fact, there are some castes which do not quite fit into any of the four *varnas*. I do not know enough about the situation in South India. But in the Northern India, castes such as Khatris and the Kayasthas are difficult to fit into the *varna* system. The Khatris are par excellence traders, but they are not classified amongst the *vaishyas*. Nor are they a part of the Kshatriyas. But their position in the caste hierarchy is well known. Similarly, there is a good deal of confusion about the *varna* status of the Kayasthas. Many sociologists, including Iravati Karve, have written about the ambivalent Kshatriya status of the Marathas. Perhaps, the position of castes in relation to the four-fold division is even less satisfactory where South India is concerned. Broadly, we might say that the position of the castes in the hierarchical scale in a region was generally less in dispute than their *varna* status. A second point which may be noted is that mobility in the *varna* status of individuals and castes is a continuous feature of Indian society. Such mobility is to be found towards all the three *varnas,* including Kshatriya and Vaishyas, not merely towards the category of Brahmans. M.N. Srinivas who had used the word "sanskritization" to denote this process, now accepts that he put too much emphasis originally on the movement of groups towards the *varna* status of Brahmans. Both Srinivas and B. Stein now emphasize not merely the process of sanskritization, but other factors, such as the position of dominant peasant and land-owning classes, political power and the production system in the process of caste mobility of groups.

Srinivas further surmises that the *varna* model became more popular during British rule. Thus, growing caste rigidity was an indirect effect of British rule.[22] The rise of the Rajputs is a classic model of *varna* mobility in the earlier period. There is a good deal of discussion regarding the origin of the Rajputs—whether they were Kshatriyas, or they were drawn from other categories in the population including indigenous tribes. Modern historians are more or less agreed that the Rajputs consisted of miscellaneous groups including shudras and tribals. Some were brahmans who took to warfare, and some were from tribes—indigenous or foreign.

Now this task of assigning a *varna* status to groups of individuals was basically the function of the brahmans. But the brahmans came in only at the stage of legitimization. Change in the social or *varna* status of a group or an individual depended on a complex of factors. An individual's status may change because he has been able to acquire ownership of land, or because he acquires a lot of money in trade or in speculation of various types, or he may be member of a group or caste which has been able to establish its political control over a certain tract of territory, and thus change its way of life.[23] Once such a change comes about in actual fact, the responsibility of the brahman is legitimization. The brahmans, it might be said, fulfill the type of role which a Vice-Chancellor in a University

[22]M.N. Srinivas. "I now realise that in both my book on Coorg religion and my 'Note on Sanskritization and Westernization' I emphasised unduly the Brahmanical model of Sanskritization and ignored the other models —Kshatriya, Vaishya and Shudra." "Sanskritization is not confined to Hindu castes but also occurs among tribal and semi-tribal groups...." (p.7).

(M.N. Srinivas, *Social Change in Modern India,* Orient Longmans, Indian ed. 1972, pp. 1-45).

See also, B. Stein, "Social Mobility and Medieval South India Hindu Sects" in J. Silverberg (ed.), *Social Mobility in Caste in India,* special issue of *Comparative Studies in Society and History.*

[23]For changes in the *varna* status of Marathas in historic times, see R.E. Enthoven, *The Tribes and Castes of Bombay,* Bombay 1922 iii. pp. 19-20, Dr. (Mrs.) I. Karve, *Maharashtra, Land and its People,* Bombay, 1968, pp. 76-77; Satish Chandra, "Social Background to the Rise of the Maharatha Movement during the 17th Century," *IESHR,* Vol. X. No.3, 1973, pp. 209-217; *Essays,* loc.cit. pp.216-223.

fulfils today. Once a person has passed his or her degree, the Vice-Chancellor awards the degree which is supposed to be the seal of legitimacy of what has actually been achieved. The legitimization of authority or ownership or status is an extremely important process throughout history, and different societies have different means of legitimization. Anthropologists have mentioned some of the cults or ceremonies to admit a child into the company of grown up men or warriors, or as medicine men. In the modern world, legislatures and courts of law legitimize relations of power and property. Thus changes in social economic and political spheres would, in turn, be reflected in the caste and *varna* status. Earlier, I drew a distinction between structural changes and what had been called developmental changes. Changes in the caste status of individuals, or the movement of castes from one *varna* status to another, did not destroy the caste system, or more correctly, what is called the four-fold division of society (*chaturvarna-vyavastha*) that the caste system permitted the movement of individuals as well as of groups or castes from one caste or *varna* status to another strengthened the system rather than weakened it. A system which was so rigid that it could not permit or take note of a changed and changing reality had to go sooner or later. It is a fallacy to think that the caste system in India has been totally rigid. It has survived so long because of its flexibility. Of course, crises of adjustment have risen at different times. At such times, social reformers, thinkers and saint-philosophers have played a distinctive role. The impact of their ideas on the caste system and the extent to which they were able to promote social change have to be studied carefully. It has to be examined whether they were the archetype of the guru mentioned by Max Weber who "implemented an established order rather than breaking it," or were men of a different mould.[24]

[24]Talcott Parson. Introduction to Max Weber's *The Sociology of Religion*, Methuen, London, 1965, p. XXXV.

Legitimization is accompanied by the process of rationalization. Without using it in the strictly Weberian sense, rationalization implied acceptance of a process of social change with reference to customs, practices and beliefs which had existed earlier and some of which, in fact, were threatened by these changes. We may see the process of rationalization in what are called the *pratilom* and the *anulom* marriages. These marriages have sought to be used as an explanation for the rise of every new caste or a sub-caste. The explanation runs: a man belonging to 'x' caste married a woman belonging to 'y' caste, from their union arose a new caste called 'z'. Then 'z' married a person from the caste 'a' and a new caste Z^1 arose, This process can repeat itself endlessly. So, the social economic and political processes are neatly disposed of and the phenomena of the rise of new caste or sub-castes appears to be as natural and mysterious as the birth of the caste system itself.

Apart from the impact of changes in relations of ownership of land, wealth and political power on the caste system, the persistence of tribes, and the interaction of the Hindu caste cum village community on these tribes are aspects which have not received the due attention of historians. As I have argued earlier, it has been shown, in my opinion quite convincingly, that the real reason why large numbers of new castes and sub-castes make their appearance in the period after the 7th century A.D. is partly because during this period Hinduism is expanding and bringing in more and more tribes into the framework of Hinduism. The process of the assimilation of the tribal people into Hinduism, implied assigning to them a definite place in the caste and *varna* hierarchy. The set belief that Hinduism has never been a proselytizing religion, that one can only be born into Hinduism, that Hinduism can only shrink, it cannot expand, is, I am afraid, not historically tenable. The process of expansion of Hinduism has gone on throughout history. In fact, it is going on even today through the process of assimilating tribal groups and giving them a definite place in the caste hierarchy. While these changes fall into the category of developmental changes, they are nevertheless, not unimportant and do have a bearing on the working of Hinduism.

A number of structural changes have taken place in Indian society since the breakdown of tribalism. The early class society was not based on slavery, the *dasas* being incorporated in village society which had its own hierarchy. Differentiation in village society was certainly one factor in the growth of what may be called feudalism. The application of the word feudalism to Indian society has been debated among Indian historians for many years. It is clear that there are many specific features of European feudalism which we do not find in India. For instance, we do not find serfdom in India in an institutional form, though large sections of the peasantry were personally dependent on, and some of them were tied to the soil. Nor do we find a manorial economy in India. But the basic features of the peasants being subjected to a superior class which did not work on the land itself and which lived on the surplus produced by the land by the peasant, and of the peasant being forced to part with a substantial part of their produce by extra economic and militaristic methods are common features. These features gradually developed within the womb of the body politic, and came more and more into prominence from the time of Harsha, particularly in the period between the 7th and 12th centuries, which is sometimes called the Rajput period in Northern India. Now if a powerful military leader emerges and he and his following start realizing the land revenue from the rural areas, it is bound to affect in one way or the other, the privileges of the peasants organized in village communities. In other words, in certain ways the rise of feudalism was an anti-thesis to the type of village community which had apparently came into existence in the post-Mahabharata War period. The growth of feudalism led to growing disparities in society. The caste system tended to become rigid because the feudal ruling class had a vested interest in not allowing others to acquire positions of power and privilege. The backing of the brahmans was necessary both to legitimize the *varna* status of the existing power groups, as well as to deny this status to their rivals. Large scale temple building activity which is a specific feature of this period marked the power and dominance of this feudal class. The brahmans who were asked to manage these temples, many of which had extensive lands and received rich gifts from the classes and the veneration of the simple folks, were direct beneficiaries. In turn, the brahmans legitimized the positions of the new class, proclaiming them as Kshatriyas, irrespective of their social background. There is some evidence that the growing social rigidity, which was one result of the close alliance between the brahmans and the feudal classes represented by the Rajputs, led to a popular reaction. The Tantrik movement and the Nathpanthi movement were, to some extent, a reflection of the lower class and peasant discontentment against the situation. Of course, there are many aspects of tantrism. Most of the tantriks were non-brahmans, and, at first, they rejected the social and intellectual framework put forward by the brahmans. Many tantrik practices reflected the fears and deep seated urges of the common people. However, tantrism tended to become more and more esoteric and retreated into a shell, as it was. As far as the Nathpanthis are concerned, most of the *siddhas* amongst the Nathpanthis were people drawn from the shudras.[25] The *siddhas* had considerable influence all over North India. The nature and impact of the *siddha* movement, the extent of their influence, the social background of the movement as also the larger question whether the *siddhas* had any role in discrediting the feudal ruling

[25]See George W. Briggs, *Gorakhnath and the Kanphata Yogis,* O.U.P., 1938, pp. 50-61; Dr. Mohan Singh, *Gorakhnath and Medieval Hindu Mysticism,* Lahore, 1937. "But thinly veiled under all accounts is the fact that Gorakh came from the lower, perhaps the lowest classes in the scale of Hindu society." (pp.23-24).

class and their brahman allies in the eyes of the people before the advent of the Turks are questions which need detailed study before any definite conclusions can be drawn.

As far as South India is concerned, the decline of Buddhism and Jainism and the rise of Adyars and Alvars who were drawn from the common people represent facets of deeper change within society. However, I do not consider myself competent to comment on these aspects. The Bhakti movement in Northern India was, to some extent, an off-shoot of this movement. Perhaps, the Bhakti movement would not have found such a ready welcome in Northern India if the Nathpanthi movement had not sown the seeds of protest against brahmans. The triumph of the Turks also dealt a mortal blow to the feudal Rajput-Brahman alliance and created an intellectual, moral, and social crisis.

The early Rajput feudalism was, to some extent, modified by the Turks. The essence of this was the *iqtadari* or the *jagirdari* system. Although the word *jagirdari* began to be used only in the Mughal period, we may use it as a generic term here. The *jagirdari* system implied that the local rulers i.e., the Rana Rawats, Thakurs etc., who had power in the rural areas, were not displaced from their positions, but the nobles, i.e., the new ruling class or the central elite assumed the responsibility of collecting the land revenue from the villages. A jagir was any defined regular source of income. Since the largest such source of income in those days was land revenue, a jagir implied assigning to the nobles responsibility for collecting land revenue from the old landed elements who had emerged to the fore-front in the post-Harsha period. Thus, the old feudal elements were not displaced but, in a certain manner, they acquired a new legitimacy. In course of time, the generic term *zamindar* began to be applied to all the elements, from rajas dominating large tracts of territory to petty village zamindars. The Mughals tried, on the one hand, to safeguard the interests of the cultivators by giving certain rights and privileges to the village community. On the other hand, for administrative convenience, certain responsibilities and tasks such as the realization of land revenue, the enforcement of local law and order etc., were vested with the local landed elements which superior rights, i.e, the zamindars. The jagirdars were placed in authority over them. This was a society in which tensions and inner contradictions were not resolved, but were papered over. Although a few rajas and zamindars were drawn into the nobility, the contradictions between the state and the zamindars, and between these and the peasant community were not resolved. However, outwardly a magnificent edifice was created. The type of centralization which the Turkish and Mughal rulers were able to achieve is remarkable. The nobles were not permitted to develop any local interests and could be moved from one part of the country to another in pursuit of imperial interests. The association of rajas and zamindars with local interests tended to go against this tradition. The feudal decentralizing tendency and the centralizing imperial tendency were perpetually contending against each other. Thus, none of the old contradictions was resolved. If anything, new contradictions were added.

The downfall of the Mughal empire and of the society which the Mughals had helped to create was an outcome of these deep-seated social contradictions. Thus, we have a picture in which tribalism had not disappeared, but the Hindu society and the village community were continuously encroaching on the tribals. Also, the village community itself was contending against the zamindar who, in turn, was contending against the jagirdar. All these contradictions were carefully maintained and utilized by the Turkish and Mughal rulers so that a powerful centralized, imperial structure could be built up.

I will not dwell at length on the second dimension, viz., the rise of a money economy which comes to prominence during the 17th century, since I have expressed my views on the subject elsewhere.[26] The development of a money economy during the period implied the growth of rich peasants and *mahajans* (money-lenders cum grain dealers) in rural society. The growth of a rich, commercial bourgeoisie and the increasing subjection of the artisans to this class and the middle-men *(dallals, gumashtas)* appointed by them and a growing desire on the part of the feudal ruling classes to use commercial profit as a supplement to their feudal incomes, thus maintaining an even higher standard of living, led to new contradictions in addition to the previous ones.

All the contradictions of Indian society came to the surface with the slackening of Imperial control during the 18th century, the growing discontentment and factionalism of the nobility who found that the Imperial system no longer suited their interests and hence strove to carve out principalities where they could function more fully as feudal barons, i.e., without the limitations of the jagirdari system. The peasants, the lower officials and the professional classes suffered, and their lament is reflected in the Urdu poetry of the time. Trade and commerce might have been affected in this situation, but traders were made welcome in many principalities, and in some of them (e.g. Bengal) they even played a role in politics. The over-all development of society towards a more highly commercialized economy or a money economy suffered a set back with the establishment of colonial rule. Through the Permanent Settlement of Bengal, the Ryotwari and Mahaldari settlements, as well as the Zamindari settlements, the British tried either to create a new class of people holding superior rights in land (Bengal), or tried to come to terms with

[26]See *Essays on Medieval Indian History*, O.U.P., 2003, pp.225-282.

the class of persons who had acquired these rights during different parts of the country during the 18th century. Thus, peasant discontent and the challenge posed by the native class of "traders could be contained at one and the same time." Preservation and reversion of the process of "re-feudalization," i.e, strengthening the dependency of peasants on those holding superior rights, and the defence of the feudal elements became a vital part of British Colonial policy. This society began to change during the second half of the nineteenth century with India entering the railway age and the growth of the national movement.

It will thus be seen that Indian society has passed through many phases. The specific features of the different phases, the factors which led to the blending of one phase into another and the potentialities and the problems posed merit careful study. The various heterodox sects and movements as well as movements of protest, dissent and reform which are a constant feature should be seen against this context and for further elucidating the internal conflicts, tensions and contradictions in our society. It is not easy to categorize which of these movements reflected the hopes and aspirations of new social classes or groups such as the artisans, the rapidly growing city population, the new commercial classes or the "bourgeoisie." Many of these were, perhaps, a reflection of the frustration of a large section of the community against what has been called their "low status" in society. The task of the historian, the sociologist, and of those who deal with various aspects of society, whether it is philosophy or literature, should be to try and make an integrated study of these various aspects so that we can arrive at a better understanding of the forces which were at work in Indian society, which were all the time changing and modifying the structure of society. The internal contradictions of this society sometimes burst into the open, but more often they were reflected in devious ways in diverse fields such as rise of religious sects generally considered remote from social, economic and political processes.

Vice-Chancellor, I would like to express my gratitude to you for having accorded me an opportunity of putting before this learned audience some of my ideas regarding the processes of social change in India, with special reference to the medieval period. I am deeply grateful to you all for having given me such a patient hearing.

CHAPTER II

Writings on, and Study of Rajasthan History

There has been growing consciousness that the history of India, particularly the history of the Indian people, cannot be understood without paying due attention to regional history and micro studies. I, therefore, welcome the growing interest in the field of regional history. Regional history congresses are being organized in a number of States such as West Bengal, Madhya Pradesh, Maharashtra, Punjab, Rajasthan, etc. This is a healthy trend as long as regional history is studies not in a narrow, parochial manner but against the background of national developments. Regions, even if they have a specificity, are not isolated. Ideas, movements and developments in one part of the country have repercussions on many other regions. As far as Rajasthan is concerned, it lies across the main routes linking the Gujarat sea ports within the Gangetic valley. Movement of goods and people across it, and hence exchange of ideas and culture was thus inevitable, and it would be doubly wrong to study Rajasthan history in isolation. I am glad that Executive Committee of the Rajasthan History Congress has never taken a narrow view of Rajasthan history and has always invited historian from all parts of the country to join in its deliberations.

The study of Rajasthan history has passed through many phases. For Col. Tod, it was primarily a study of chivalrous deeds by a band of people who would almost be equated to the English feudal aristocracy. Tod's writing had two aspects—political and social. The political aspect was carried further by Kaviraj Shyamaldas, Pt. Ram Karan Asopa, Gauri Shankar Hira Shankar Ojha, Pt. Vishveshwarnath Reu and a galaxy of eminent historians whom I cannot list in detail due to shortage of time. Many monographs have been published on the subject in various universities. Unfortunately, not all of them have been published so far. The published monographs, where Rajasthani records have been checked with Persian sources, are a useful addition to our knowledge.

The nature of the Mughal-Rajput relations has been an abiding topic of interest, and a number of detailed works have been produced on the subject. Amongst the earliest of these was Dr. Gopi Nath Sharma's book *Relations of Mewar with the Mughal Emperors*. Relations of Marwar with the Mughal Emperors have been studied by Dr. V.S. Bhargava, and of Bikaner by Dr. Karni Singh. Dr. M.L. Sharma's book on the Kotah State has, to some extent, also covered its relations with the Mughal Emperors. Although a few gaps remain, the political aspects of the relationship of the Rajput rajas with the Mughal empire, have been covered in fair detail. Dr. V. S. Bhatnagar's recent monograph on *Sawai Jai Singh and His Times* which I have read with interest, has covered the first half of the 18th century. These studies have shown that the Rajput relationship with the Mughals was not a one-sided one, but was based on mutual advantage. The alliance helped the Mughal Emperors to meet the challenge faced by them from a section of disaffected and ambitious nobles, and in consolidating an empire based on liberal principles, such as religious toleration, equal opportunity in service to various ethnic and religious groups, etc. The Rajput rajas on the other hand, were provided an opportunity for holding a variety of important positions and posts in far-flung parts of the empire. Imperial help and backing also enabled them to strengthen their internal position. The

Mughal Emperors claimed the right to regulate and recognize the succession, and there are a number of cases on record when they even set aside the nomination of a ruler. But such occurrences were not numerous. The process of succession which had often led to fratricidal conflict was, on the whole, orderly. Nor were the inter-state rivalries among the Rajput States allowed to get out of hand. The long era of peace which Rajasthan enjoyed along with the rest of the country, and the growth of trade and commerce, benefited the rulers in other ways as well—a point which they became painfully aware of in the 18th century when the decline of Mughal power led to renewed internecine warfare and the incursion of the Marathas into Rajasthan. The Marwar war of 1678 with Aurangzeb formed a kind of a water-shed, and it seems that important changes in the Rajput political structure can be traced back from it. Till 1678, many leading Rajput rajas received large jagirs in addition to their *watan*. In the case of Jaswant Singh, who held the mansab of 7000 zat, 7000 sawars *du-aspahsih-aspah,* the income from the Mughal jagirs was almost as large as the income from his *watan*. Jagirs granted in the area considered the *watan* of the Rajputs were not transferred during the life time of a raja. Both Raja Gaj Singh and Maharaja Jaswant Singh were granted only three parganas in Marwar at the time of their accession. Other parganas were granted to them in due course as their mansabs were increased. Thus the *watan* of a Raja was itself a variable one. The jagirs outside the *watan* were transferable as in the case of any other Imperial mansabdar. The details and the amounts of the jagirs have been mentioned by Nainsi, and have been checked with other sources by Dr. G.D. Sharma in his thesis *Politics and Administration in the State of Marwar 1638-1749*. He has shown that, while the income from jagirs outside Marwar never exceeded that from jagirs in Marwar, the income from the former was not inconsiderable—varying from 1.17 crores to 5.39 crores *dams*. In the case of the rulers of Jaipur, whose *watan* was smaller, the proportion granted in jagir outside their *watan* must have been larger. A clearer picture would emerge only after scholars have been allowed to scrutinize in detail the records held by the Maharaja of Jaipur in his personal custody. The same applies to the records in the custody of the Maharan of Mewar.

The nature of the *watan* held by the rulers of Jodhpur and Jaipur, has some other interesting features. In the case of the rulers of Marwar, even in the pargana of Jodhpur, Raja Udai Singh was granted only *14 tappas* with a *jama* of Rs. 10.47 lakhs, whereas Raja Sur Singh was granted *18 tappas* with a *jama* of Rs. 16.92 lakhs (approximately). In other words, even within the *watans* of the Rajas, a number of *tappas* and villages were either administered directly by the Mughal emperors, or assigned to jagirdars. I had made a brief comment on this in an article written for the *Comprehensive History of India in 1970.* The article has yet to be published,* but since then, both Shri G.D. Sharma and Shri S.P. Gupta of the Aligarh Muslim University have established this point with full statistics on the basis of village and pargana records of Eastern Rajasthan. Thus, it would appear that the Mughal control over the territories of the Rajput rajas could be very considerable as long as the jagirdari system worked effectively. As soon as it broke down, the jagirdars holding small jagirs in the *watan* of the Rajputs had no option but to let them out on *ijara* to the Rajput rajas.

The alliance between the Mughals and the Rajputs was an alliance between two ruling groups, each of which was rooted in a distinctive socio-economic background, and had their own ethos, political ideals and objectives. The alliance between the two was, therefore, subject to many

*Published I.H.R. IV, 1978 pp.326-33, I.H.R. V. Nos.1-2, 1978-79, pp.135-51, and in *Essays on Medieval Indian History*, pp. 357-445.

strains—political, social, cultural, etc. It is unfortunate that excessive emphasis on and preoccupation with the matrimonial aspect of the alliance between the Mughals and the Rajput Rajas had led to a neglect of the other aspects. A careful study of the stresses and strains in the Mughal Rajput alliance—its development, its social, political and cultural aspect is highly desirable. I had tried to underline some of the social and political aspects in my article written in 1970. But many more detailed studies dealing with various aspects of alliance will be needed before all the various aspects of the alliance are grasped.

Hardly any detailed work has been done so far on the internal administration of the Rajput states, and the nature of the relationship between the various Rajput states during Mughal rule. That there were many inner tensions among the Rajputs and between the leading states is well known. The Mughals were not unaware of them and utilized them for their purposes whenever necessary. Thus, in 1574, Akbar placed Jodhpur under Raja Rai Singh of Bikaner. Pokharan and Satalmer was always a bone of contention between Marwar and Bikaner. There was tensions between Marwar and Mewar also about Gorwar. Hardly any study has been made of the position of different Rajput clans in individual states, their relationship with each other, and with the Raja. A careful study of the *patta* system, the *thikanedari* system, and the working of the revenue system in the Rajput states is necessary in order to help us to understand the nature and evolution of Rajasthan society during the medieval period. Unless this is done with the help of documents, the discussion about “feudalism” in Rajasthan might degenerate into an exercise in logic chopping and semantics. Some of the young scholars, such as G.D. Sharma, S.P. Gupta and Dilbagh Singh, etc., who have made critical study of pargana and village records, have contributed to a better understanding of specific aspects of Rajput society and administration. I look forward to many more studies of this nature.

Of late there has been growing interest in the social and economic history of India. The massive documentary material available in Rajasthan which runs into millions of documents is almost unique in its range, variety and richness. It is an invaluable source of information not only for the economic and administrative history of Rajasthan, but has relevance to the country as a whole. It is hardly necessary for me to recall that it was Sir Jadunath Sarkar, the doyen of medieval Indian history, who first drew the attention of the scholars to the mass of documentary material lodged in the Jaipur State Archives. It was due largely to his untiring efforts that the *Persian Akhbarat* which was a unique source of information from the middle of the 17th century onwards could be make available to the historical world. However, it is only in the last decade or so and after the records from the various states have been centralized at the Rajasthan State Archives, Bikaner that historians have been enabled to utilize the other documentary material which is several times more voluminous than the *Akhbarat* and which had remained largely unknown and inaccessible to Sir Jadunath. If I may be permitted to strike a personal note, the first list of the *arhsattahs* lodged in the Jaipur State Archives was prepared for my benefit in 1959. Neither the contents nor the nature of these documents were known at the time; in fact they were sometimes called *atha-sathas*, i.e., documents containing eight knots dealing with miscellaneous topics. At my instance, Shri Satya Prakash Gupta of the Aligarh Muslim University abstracted a full copy of some of the *arhsattas* which I analyzed and in collaboration with S.P. Gupta presented it in the form of a paper in 1964[1] Subsequently,

[1]Published as Jaipur Pargana records in the Indian Economic and Social History review, Vol. VI, No. 3, September 1966, pp. 303-315.

professor Nurul Hasan in collaboration with S.P. Gupta, presented a paper on "The prices of Food Grains in the Territories of Amber" based on *arhsattas.*[2] Since then a large number of other documents, such as *syaha mujmil, nirakh bazaar, dastur-ul-amal*, and other records dealing with revenue administration have become available, and are being used for a detailed study of the trend of the cropping and price pattern, growth of agricultural production, village stratification, etc., in eastern Rajasthan. Statistical studies of this kind have helped to take the study of medieval India to an altogether higher plane. Even though time series are not available, sophisticated mathematical models and use of the computer for analyzing documentary material has yielded information vital for understanding the pattern of agricultural production and the broad economy in India during the 17th and 18th centuries. Some of these detailed studies with which I have been associated, will, I hope, be published soon. Broadly speaking, while there was a marked rise of prices during the 18th century over the 17th, there appears to be remarkable stability in rents and production till the middle of the 18th century. I had argued earlier in my book, *Parties and Politics*, that the great anarchy on which English historians laid so much emphasis in the general context of the 18th century and which was used by them as a kind of justification for the British conquest of India was, in fact, confined to very narrow tracts of the country, generally far removed from the political centers of gravity of India, and only for a short period during the second half of the 18th century while new emerging states had not stabilized. To some extent the detailed economic trends in eastern Rajasthan appear to support my contention. But a final conclusion can only be arrived at when such statistical studies can be carried out for different parts of the country as well.

[2]Procs. I.H.C., Mysore, 1966.

The unique importance of the Rajasthani records for the social, economic and administrative history of India during the medieval period should be clear from the foregoing remarks. I am, therefore, rather concerned at the neglect of languages in our syllabi in various universities. While the study of the English has its own importance, it obviously plays only a marginal role in the study of the evolution of our society and culture till the arrival of the British. Even during British rule, the study of records in regional languages is of great importance for the historian, particularly if we want to shift the focus of our study from British policies to the life and culture of the Indian people. A number of useful monographs and thesis have been written on political and administrative aspects of the Rajput states during the 19th century. There is a mass of material for studying the development of society and the economy during the period. It is, therefore, regrettable that hardly any of the universities in Rajasthan have a provision for giving training in the various dialects and scripts of Rajasthan without a knowledge of which the records can hardly be utilized. In the same manner, the study of the Persian language and script which is essential since in the Rajasthani documents as well as in the Marathi revenue documents of the period innumerable Persian terms and expression are used is being neglected. I hope that in some of the universities in Rajasthan as well as outside it, due attention will be paid to the study of the various languages in which documentary material is contained, viz., Persian, Rajasthani, medieval Marathi, etc.

The universities should also pay greater attention to the calendaring and indexing of documents. In view of the large numbers of the documents and the meager staff and resources, it may not be possible for the Rajasthan State Archives authorities to undertake single handed the indexing and calendaring of the huge mass of documents in their custody. I wonder whether it is possible for the universities to amend their ordinances in such a manner as to enable a student to get his Ph.D. degree on the basis of preparing an index or calendar of certain number of documents or documents of a particular type. Of course, the index must contain appropriate footnotes and a brief summary as well as a scholarly introduction. The Indian Historical Records Commission has suggested this to the universities more than once. Unfortunately not many universities have cared to take up the suggestion so far. I wonder whether Universities in Rajasthan would take a lead in the matter. In addition to this, it is essential to publish the other material pertaining to Rajasthan history. Hardly any of the *Khyats* have been published so far. I am glad that with the assistance of the Indian Council of Historical Research, Dr. G.N. Sharma has undertaken editing and publication of Mewar *Khyats*. I have, in association with Maharajkumar Raghubir Singh and G.D. Sharma, edited and published the *Hukmat ri-Bahi* . Shri Narayan Singh Bhati's contributions in the field are well known. But these efforts need to be greatly augmented.

Lastly, I consider it incumbent upon the universities particularly those located in the State of Rajasthan, to undertake an intensive effort for the location, indexing and preservation of private papers. It is well known that various *thikanedars* have large collections of private papers. Some of these are already in an advanced state of decay and may be lost if proper efforts are not made to use them and to calendar them. Apart from the universities, other organizations such as the Indian Council of Historical Research could also play a role. At the instance of the Council, Dr. V.S. Bhargava, has already undertaken the task of indexing and calendaring of the documents in the possession of Rao Sahib Masooda. I hope, more such enlightened *thikanedars* would throw their records open to scholars. This would help avoiding in Rajasthan the criminal destruction of old records which has taken place in a number of other states. The University Grants Commission has been inviting research proposals from scholars both in the field of natural science as well as in the field of social sciences and humanities. I am quite sure that the listing, collection and calendaring of historical documents, material objects, literary works, etc., would certainly receive support form the Commission in the prescribed manner. The Universities might also send proposals for archaeology for which there is so much scope in Rajasthan, and for the study of arty history, medieval architecture, etc. Historical geography is another neglected field.

CHAPTER III

Some Aspects of Urbanization in Medieval India

The study of urban centers and urbanization in India is a part and parcel of the growing recent interest in economic and social history of India. In the 1950s, when I was at Aligarh, a Ph.D. thesis had been prepared under the supervision of Professor Sheikh Abdul Rashid. I was indirectly associated, because the researcher (I.P. Gupta) had been my former student at Allahabad and frequently consulted me. An interesting point which emerged from that study was that the concept of Bernier that Indian cities were merely military camps was not supported by the evidence at our disposal. Another interesting conclusion which emerged was that the extent of urbanization in India during the 17th century was much higher than what it was in British India at the beginning of the century. The thesis unfortunately has not been published till now, but I recall that the percentage of the urban population in Northern India worked out to over 15 per cent. Recently, Professor Irfan Habib has worked out a figure of about 12½ to 15 per cent for the urban centers in Mughal India.

Not only Bernier's statement, but unfortunately, the repetition of the idea by Marx in his letters that the cities in India were mere military camps has for long become a barrier in the growth of urban studies in India. Even now perhaps, we have not been able to cross over it completely. Some of our notions rest on the models of economic and urban growth put forward in Europe in the 1940s. I have in mind the model of the development of Medieval Europe put forward by Henry Pirenne in which he postulated that towns grow with the growth of trade, particularly long distance trade, and secondly, that the entire development of society, the growth of a new social order, the capitalist order, is predicated on a kind of division of labour between the cities and the towns, industry or handicrafts being concentrated largely in the towns and the countryside merely supplying the raw materials and the food stuffs. In other words, he postulated what might be called a kind of an internal colonial structure where the dynamic developmental factors were concentrated in the towns and the peasants merely were, as Leon Trotsky once observed, 'the pack mules of history.'

The role of agricultural production was largely ignored in this model. In fact, it was virtually assumed that agricultural productivity remained static during the medieval age. Also demographic factors were not taken into account. With much greater information on medieval times, both the agricultural and the demographic factors have been woven into the new studies in the West. Writers such as Guy Bois have shown that demography and prices had a direct effect on expansion of land under cultivation, with productivity declining on account of marginal lands being brought under cultivation. According to him, when population outstripped production, famines reduced population, land fell out of cultivation and productivity rose. This cyclic movement had a direct impact on urban population and urban industry. In some of the early Western writings on India, the fact that the towns were not the foci of industry has been emphasized. That in India the towns did not have a separate juridical entity, like the towns in Europe, was used as another argument to prove that the towns in India were merely exploiters or parasitic, thus underlining that the totally stagnant oriental society as a whole was incapable of developing. When we look at the processes of development of our society, we have first to discard these ideas and models which have been set aside in the West but unfortunately continue to influence thinking in our country.

We are now moving away from excessive dependence on long distance trade as a vehicle of social and economic change. This point has been brought out well by Dr. Nandi in his Presidential Address to the Ancient Indian History Section of the Indian History Congress in 1984. Dr. Nandi has pointed out that the towns in India started reviving in the eleventh century, and that feudalization in the early period did mean a considerable growth of agriculture. This has implications which need careful thinking. At the outset, let me say that if you do not like the word feudalism, you are welcome to use some other term as long as we are clear about the basic concept. What I imply by feudalism is a society in which the cultivator is exploited by extra economic means, by a class of people who do not work on the land themselves. Whether this exploitation had a tendency to inhibit increase of production is an arguable point. Quite obviously, exploitation could increase without production growing simultaneously. So, when we try to understand the process of the growth of towns, or the lack of such a process, the growth of agricultural production, the manner in which agricultural surplus is distributed, the structure of the village society, the development as well as the inhibiting factors, all become important. What precise role the growth or decline of long distance trade plays in the process needs detailed examination.

Professor R. S. Sharma has argued in his extremely valuable thesis on feudalism in India, that growth of localism was linked on the one hand with the process of giving grants of land to the brahmans, and political decentralization, and on the other with the decline of long distance trade. He has further traced the absence of gold coins in North India between the 7th and 10th centuries to decline of long distance north-south trade in India. Perhaps this thesis needs some modification because there does not seem to have been a decline of town life all over India during the period. While some of the bigger town declined, the extent of the decline of town life during the period in South India in particular is a moot question.

In his address, Dr. Nandi had emphasized the decline of coin of small value. Quite obviously, coins of small value had much greater importance for the smaller towns, for local trade and local transactions rather than for long distance trade. When did the process of urban revival begin? With the arrival of the Turks in the 13th century, or earlier, in the 11th? The arrival of the Turks helped in the process of political integration by breaking down localism, and they helped in opening overland commerce between India, Central Asia and Western Asia. These were important factors in the process of the growth of towns in India in the 13th and 14th centuries. If, however, the process of the revival of towns starts not in the 13th century but in the 11th century, the entire matter would have to be re-considered. The question is important, because it is possible to argue that historians have a tendency to link political disintegration too closely with economic processes, such as the towns and town life. The argument that the period before the arrival of the Turks in India was one of political disintegration, and, therefore, one during which the growth of towns was not possible, can be equally applied to the period after the decline of the Tughlaq Empire, i.e., the 15th century. This was, in general, a period of political disintegration, especially in North India. But I am somewhat doubtful of its also being a period of the decline of towns. The Sultanate of Delhi shrank to half of its former size under Firoz Tughlaq. Yet there is no shrinkage of towns; the period witnessed in fact the establishment of many new towns. It is clear that the entire growth of towns during the period of Firoz Tughlaq is closely linked with agricultural expansion, with the canal network, the improvement of horticulture and the establishment of large numbers of orchards all around the towns. I suppose that the development of orchards and horticulture in the neighbourhood of Delhi would not have been possible without assured supply of water. Even today, if anybody has anything to do with the development of orchards in areas near Delhi, assured supply of water is essential. So, attention to supply of water for irrigation, either through canals or through wells, was a very important development. This applied not only to the Sultanat which helped to popularize a more efficient type of water-wheel (*arhatta*) but also the Provincial Kingdom which laid considerable emphasis on agriculture. The role of the Afghans in the agricultural expansion also needs to be rethought. We have tended to dismiss the Afghans as merely barbarians, as people who were mercenaries of one category of warlords or the other. But the very fact that the Afghans, as distinct from the Turks, settled in the countryside suggests that they must have had something more to do with agriculture, not merely as people who in one way or the other extracted surplus. Thus, if we are to broaden our earlier understanding, and link the growth of towns not only with the growth of trade and industry, but also with the growth of agriculture, the so-called period of decline and disintegration would perhaps emerge in a new light.

This would be equally applicable to the 18th century. Just as the 15th century is projected as a period of disintegration and decline, because of the downfall of the Delhi Sultanat, the 18th century has traditionally been presented as a period of disintegration, in which urban life registered a precipitate decline. I have argued elsewhere that even in the context of large towns, such as Agra and Delhi, we have been too much influenced by the literary outpourings of Urdu poets such as Sauda. The *Shahr Ashob* in which Sauda lamented the decline of Delhi is not as much a reflection of reality as we have been inclined to believe. The entire tradition of *Shahr Ashob* was a literary device, and as early as in the middle of the 17th century, we find the practice of writing *Shahr Ashob* where the poet wrote of the decline of handicrafts, rise of unworthy incompetent people, and the low castes. This tradition continued. A stray remark of the author *of the Ma'asir-ul-Umara* in 1772 shows that Delhi was a very flourishing city and that all kinds of arts and crafts were practiced there. What do we do when we are faced with diametrically opposite evidence? We try to strike a balance. There certainly was a decline of Delhi. But what type of decline, is a point which needs to be studied because there is no one-to-one relationship. It does not mean that as soon as a city ceases to be an administrative capital, it declines. A great deal depends upon the basis upon which a city was first selected or emerged as an administrative centre. Whether it had an agricultural hinterland, the advantage of communications, and so on and so forth.

Another point relates to small towns and their study on a regional basis. Quite obviously, the pattern of small towns would differ from region to region and also from area to area. The growth of *qasbas* in the 16th and 17th centuries is emphasized. Moreover, whereas in the Sultanat period a *qasba* was a village with a fort, in the 16th-17th centuries, a *qasba* was a village with a market. So the entire concept of the *qasba* changed during the period. How and why we do not know. Regarding the distribution of the *qasbas* distance-wise, the study of the communication network is very useful in this process. We know that the distribution of towns in their spatial dimensions varied considerably from area to area. Throughout the medieval period, there was a maximum distance which the travellers who used horses or oxen normally traveled. Within a distance from ten to twelve miles, there had to be a place where they could stay. This meant a *sarai* or a substantial village, or a *qasba* or some such place. In many cases, *the sarai* were either located in the *qasba* or subsequently *qasbas* developed around them. Quite obviously this does not apply equally to every area. For instance, I do not think that the distribution of *qasbas* in Rajasthan could match the distribution of *qasbas* in the Ganga-Jamuna Doab.

The third point which I think needs to be studied is the cultural role of the towns. I think we should not consider the cultural aspect to be unimportant. For instance, we, always talk of a Delhi culture or of a Lucknow culture. The manner in which these cultures developed is a matter which needs detailed study. I have pointed out elsewhere that even an orthodox ruler like Aurangzeb was not able to suppress the liberal integrationist aspects of Delhi culture. When Aurangzeb went to the South, he sent his daughter Zeb-un-Nisa to Delhi. Zeb-un-Nisa soon set up a centre (*Bait-ul-Ulum*) at Delhi for poets and others who continued the old tradition of liberal integrationist studies. What is more important is that the type of the people who were involved in the centre were not merely the nobles, but people drawn from a much broader strata, the middle class. The economic role of the middle classes has been studied by some scholars including Dr. Iqtidar Alam Khan. To what extent was the middle class able to provide a cultural ethos also? Perhaps this might be linked with the fact that many of the nobles built *mandis* and had their own orchards. Thus, they and their descendents no longer depended upon the patronage of the government. They could live even if they were denied a *jagir* or a *mansab,* or if the yield of one had dried up. It was this class which kept life in the city going and provided backing and support to cultural life.

The last point I would like to make is about the neglected role of the Marathas. I do not think that any careful study has so far been done about the role of the Marathas in relation to the process of urbanization. The development of Poona alone does not signify a growing process of urbanization. Even though the hoarded wealth of nobles, *sahukars* etc. all over the Mughal empire was flowing into the Maratha coffers through the process of plunder, we do not see any outburst of manufacturing industries or the arts. The armaments of the Maratha army remained primitive. The Maratha cavalrymen were supposed to be armed only with a spear. Even later, they did not acquire the type of musket which had been developed and was being used by the Afghans. In fact, it was the musket firing Afghan infantry which was able to repel the Maratha onslaught at Shukar-tal (1752). Contemporary British writers have pointed to the rather primitive nature of the Maratha artillery. Does it mean that the Marathas did not have a strong base of metallurgy, since a strong tradition of metallurgy could only have been provided by the towns. In other words, a low level of urbanization, or poorly developed artisanal base, particularly in metallurgy, had a much more significant long range effect on the Marathas than has been postulated so far. To an extent, this was closely linked to the position of the small towns because the small towns not only acted as markets and centres of sale of agricultural produce but also developed as centres of handicrafts. The metallurgical base of the small towns in the Upper Ganga Valley enabled the Afghan soldiers to be equipped with muskets as also their other requirements.

These are some of the points which need deeper study. Such a study can be made only if we use the records in various regions of the country. We are all extremely eager to develop regional studies. But if all we do in the name of regional study is merely to try and project local heroes to the national level, I am afraid we neither do any service to the cause of national integration nor arrive at a better understanding of the process of the development of our society. Since we are meeting in South India, in one of its cultural centres located in an extremely rich agricultural hinterland and one which has always had extensive overland and overseas trade links (Calicut), I hope that some young scholars of the region would undertake an intensive study of the process of urbanization in the region and answer some of the questions I have broached here.

CHAPTER IV

Why did an Industrial Revolution not Take Place in India

It is generally agreed that by the end of the 17th century, India was producing a considerable amount of commodities, both industrial and agricultural, for the national and international market. Even at the time of the establishment of the Mughal empire, the Indian economy was by no means a simple natural economy having passed through a long process of commodity production from the early Christian centuries, with growth of towns and urban production. The Mughal administrative and revenue policies (peace, the development of communication, stable currency, realization of the bulk of the land revenue in cash, encouragement of cash-crops and efforts to expand cultivation etc.), and the growth of big towns and *qasbahs* in the 17th century which is amply testified to by foreign travelers, further encouraged the process. In order to discuss whether India as a whole, or any region within it was near the "take off" stage of an industrial Revolution in the $17^{th}/18^{th}$ centuries, the following aspects may be discussed: (i) the rural/ urban relationship, (ii) nature and volume of foreign and domestic commerce, (iii) organization of industry, and (iv) state of science and technology.

I. *RURAL / URBAN RELATIONSHIP*

A careful study of the Mughal agrarian system suggests that there was considerable trade between the towns and the country-side – both in food grains and the raw materials needed for urban manufacture (Irfan Habib). The ability of the countryside to feed the growing population in the towns (as well as the normal growth of population which took place, despite natural checks, such as famine and pestilence), and to cope with the growing demand of raw materials for manufacture was a favourable factor for the development of the manufacturing sector. While the village situation limited the scope of urban exports, the complete self-sufficiency of the Indian village is a myth-especially in the developing regions.

The rapid growth of towns and urban centers in India during the 17th century was the most significant factor. There is no evidence to support the contention of Bernier that the towns were merely "armed camps." Apart from being administrative and military centers, they provided a market (which also effected the rural areas) and in course of time many of them developed into centers of manufacture. As Irfan Habib has shown, urbanization in North India was about twenty per cent—not less than what existed in the same area at the beginning of the 20th century. The regional distribution of the growth of towns suggests that in the areas of Gujarat, the Malabar, Coromandel coast area, a narrow strip along the Ganges in Bengal urbanization was the result of foreign and coastal trade. However, the development of the north-west area of the Doab was due more to political factors (extraction of tribute), and growth of internal trade, although overland trade was also a factor.

The importance of the regional factor in the growth of rural-urban relationship is important. India being of continental size, it is unreal to except similar or simultaneous development all over the country (cf. Moreland). In Europe also, industrial production was concentrated in only a few regions. Gujarat and the Malabar-Coromandel coast were the most rapidly developing regions due to favourable situation such as a rich hinterland etc. Bengal came up during the second half of the 17th century. These were the areas of further potential growth.

II. *NATURE AND VOLUME OF FOREIGN AND INLAND TRADE*

It is difficult to calculate it in quantitative terms, but it was considerable according to contemporary standards. Importance of textile production for foreign commerce and growth of money-economy in India is obvious. Slow price rise despite influx of gold and silver suggests a constant rise of production. Likewise, there was considerable trade of food grains locally and on a regional basis. The growth of merchant capital testified to by (a) developed financial institutions, with something like a national finance market; (b) availability of considerable amount of liquid money at reasonable rates (Irfan Habib); (c) penetration of production especially in textile production, mining and metallurgy etc. by merchant capital via the *dadani* or putting out system. This, of course, worsened the condition of the artisans who, as Marx (*Capital*, Moscow 1957, III p. 329) has pointed out, received only their wage labour, despite owning their means of production. Nor did it mean that the "merchant capitalist" was interested in developing new techniques of production.

Probably the highest development of the economy was in Gujarat where food grains imported in large quantities suggests growth of towns which outstripped local supply of food grains. Another factor was rural areas shifting to cash crops to meet growing demand for industrial raw materials. The food grains (rice) was imported from the Coromondal Coast, Malabar as also from Bengal.

III. *ORGANIZATION OF INDUSTRY*

Textile production was located partly in towns, partly in villages in which skilled craftsmen were employed for bleaching, dyeing and printing, probably in towns under skilled or master craftsmen. Metallurgy, was also an urban craft. The position and role of master craftsmen is clear. Did Islam in India improve his position? Relationship of artisans to heterodox religions or social reform movements, and Abul Fazl's classification of artificers with merchants, next to warriors was index of a new reality (cf. remarks of Bernier).

IV. *ROLE OF SCIENCE AND TECHNOLOGY*

Not markedly backward during 16th century, but markedly so by 18th century. Was this due to intellectual climate (rise of mystic irrational movements? Were these movements useful politically, but harmful otherwise?) Nature of Mughal ruling class (feudal, or inimical to investment), caste society (premium on hereditary occupation), or Indian hostility to all foreign ideas are some of the questions to be discussed. Further questions are: (a) What was the extent and speed to which India assimilated Greco-Arabian science on the basis of which Western science developed? (b) Did India show any capacity to develop science and technology during the period? (cf. A.J. Qaiser and others on the subject).

The first needs careful investigation. Some growth of science and technology during 16th-17th centuries is shown by growth of metallurgy particularly of guns and muskets, ship building; mathematics and astronomy (improvement of the *Zich-i-Ulugh Khani*). State of optics was uncertain, despite large scale import of spectacles. Could this suffice as a sufficient basis of an Industrial Revolution or technological growth in India?

CONCLUSION

While it is hazardous to make any definite statement in the present state of our knowledge, a hypothesis may be put forward that Gujarat, at any rate, was near a "take off" stage, or had attained what has been called the first stage of capitalist growth (Growth of merchant capital). I do not know enough about conditions in the Malabar-Coromandel coastal area, but conditions there may have been similar. Despite the growing backwardness of Indian science and the social restraints imposed by Hindu society on the artisans, a new urban relationship had developed in Gujarat, with the towns emerging as centre of export industry and the rural areas adjusting themselves to the needs of the market. Despite the fall of the Mughal Empire and the Maratha depredations in the area, foreign trade of Gujarat did not decline appreciably till the second half of the 18th century. The textile industry, in particular, remained strong enough to create a serious problem for the wool manufacturers of Britain and the mercantilists during the first quarter of the 18th century. The British conquest not only upset the internal trade of the country, but gradually reversed and destroyed India's foreign trade. It also provided for the first time, free alienability of land. Combined with ruination of domestic and foreign trade, it diverted capital into purchase of land and led to what may be called "a feudal reversion" from which India struggled to free itself from the latter part of the 19th century.

P.S:

This paper, presented in 1968, has been quoted but is being printed for the first time. It was meant to chart out new pathways of research on social and economic history of medieval India, focussing on the question whether there were potentialities of growth in the economy of medieval India after the 17th century? The question has become embroiled in two other debates: factors leading to the collapse of the Mughal empire, and whether potentialities of growth meant growth of a capitalist economy? It is hardly possible to dwell on these controversies here. In brief, three points of view have emerged: (i) that given the social and economic, technological and political infrastructure of the Mughal empire, there were no possibilities of further growth, or growth of a capitalist society; (ii) that growth had continued into the 18th century, particularly in some of the new regional entities which had access to the sea, though the direction of the growth is not clear and was aborted with the establishment of British colonial rule; (iii) that a new class of "portfolio capitalists" or an intermediate section was growing in India during the 18th century which coincided with the interests of the East India Company, the growth of capitalism being adversely effected only in the 19th century.

More work is needed to resolve these issues. However, the stark and continued poverty of large masses should not be counter posed to growth. As has been argued by me elsewhere, in the rural areas, growth was fostered by the richer section of the *khud, kashta* cultivators, the zamindars and the state working largely though not exclusively through the *jagirdars* by providing resources, capital and labour. In the cities, the merchants and mater-craftsmen expanded handicraft production of various types and provided capital. However, the fruits of expansion were, as is often the case, appropriated by these sections, leaving the bulk of the cultivators and artisans as they were before, i.e, at the verge of subsistence.

(SC, 2007)

CHAPTER V

Problems of Change and Development in India—in History and under Freedom*

Indian culture which is amongst the ancient surviving indigenous cultures of Asia has demonstrated a remarkable capacity to survive and to renew itself when faced with a challenge. The capacity to maintain a continuity of tradition and, at the same time, to assimilate "external" elements and achieve a new synthesis is a typical feature of many ancient civilizations. However, little attempt has so far been made to study the mechanics of this process in detail. The caste system and religion have sometimes been assigned leading roles in this process in India. In this context, the mechanics of the absorption of tribal elements within the Hindu fold—a process which has continued down the ages and is still not at an end, has been studied by social anthropologists, and reveals that the process adjusted itself to the level of the development of the tribe: where a tribe had reached the state of economic and social differentiation, the upper elements were assigned the status of brahmans and *kshatriyas* (warriors) and the rest *shudras*; if it remained at a low level, the tribe as a whole was accorded the status of *shudras*. It was rare, as in the case of a conquering tribe such as the Rajputs, where the entire tribe was accorded the status of *kshatriyas*. At the practical level, Hinduized professional groups and

*Part of a UNESCO project on Change and Development, 1984.

castes were allowed to follow their own customs and customary laws. This accounts for the palimsest character of Indian culture.

Although the roots of Indian culture go back to the third millennium B.C., many of the features characteristic of Brahmanism, viz. the caste system, the Hindu pantheon, the doctrine of transmigration, and its characteristic way of life (the *ashram* system), began to be defined between the 8th and the 2nd century B.C. After a period of confusion marked by stagnation and decline in some branches of life which were brought about by political disintegration and foreign (Greek, Scythian) invasions, a new phase began towards the beginning of the 4th century A.D. which lasted for about 200 years. During this period, Indian society and culture received a definite mould. Thus, the *varna* or the caste system arrived at its characteristic four-fold division. The vaishyas who had evolved out of the cultivating classes into those who occupied themselves mainly with trade, commerce and banking were accorded an upper caste status. Earlier, only the brahmans and *kshatriyas* were entitled to it and were called *dvija* or twice-born.

Economically, this was a period of growth, both in the field of agriculture and handicrafts. The art of metallurgy, as testified to by the Allahabad and Mehrauli iron-pillars, seems to have attained a high level, as also shipbuilding. Buddhist remnants in Central Asia suggest a keen over-land trade, joining the trade on the "silk route" to China, while the discovery of hoards of Roman gold coins in South Indian port towns suggests an active trade with the Roman Empire. The emergence of large, stable states in the country, including South India promoted long distance internal trade, with trade-guilds (*shrenis*) playing an active role.

Economic growth was reflected in the survival of science, a leading role in the field of astronomy and mathematics being played by Aryabhatta, Bhaskara-I and Varahamihira. Medicine and Chemistry also registered a growth, the name of

Nagarjuna being associated especially with the latter. Philosophy saw vigorous debates between the Buddhists and the Brahmans with the growth of popular cults (*tantrism*) on the one hand, and highly speculative, imminantive philosophy, the *Vedanta*, on the other. There was an outburst of literary activity, with the Sanskrit poet and dramatist, Kalidasa, leading the way. The epics, *Mahabharata* and *Ramayana*, which have deeply influenced secular Indian conduct, wcrc finally amended during this period. There was vigorous activity in the writing of *dharmashastras* and *puranas* viz. religious law (which included polity) and traditions (including genealogical tables of kings). Painting and sculpture also reached a high level.

The village community too received its characteristic stamp. The service-castes consisting of the priest, the shopkeeper, the boundary-man, goldsmith-cum-moneychanger, on the one hand, and the tanner, the iron-smith, the carpenter etc., on the other, became integral parts of the village society and were assigned definite proportions of the food grains production in return for their services. Although the villages were largely self-sufficient, combining agriculture with rudimentary handicrafts, it would be wrong to consider them as being isolated from the outside world or from each other. The village shop-keeper, internal traders, wandering saints (*yogis*) and mendicants, periodic fairs and festivals, pilgrimages to holy places etc. bound the villages into a social and cultural network. The system of collecting land revenue presumed a politico-administrative network. However, absence of any large system of canals in India and the need to regulate the supply of water from wells and ponds made for a high degree of decentralization. In this context, caste provided a basis for interaction beyond the village. Groups of villages—ten, twenty, or eighty-four—were often tied to each other by ties of caste and kinship (each caste being an endogamous group, excluding marriage between prohibited categories of blood relations). Religion not only legitimized caste, but tried to smoothen relations by prescribing the duties of the various castes and in the process, establishing a hierarchy among them. Also, local cult figures were sought to be assimilated in the Hindu pantheon in some kind of a hierarchical order.

It was this complex socio-cultural order which enabled the gradual absorption and assimilation of a large number of tribes into the Aryan-Dravidian cultural system. Many of the foreign tribal elements which entered India during this period were also Hinduized in a similar manner.

The early centuries of the Christian era was a period of all round growth in India. We have already referred to the growth of metallurgy and shipbuilding. Indian handicrafts especially textiles formed the basis for an extensive overseas trade to the countries of South-East Asia (Java, Sumatra, Malay peninsula, etc.) and both overseas and overland to the West and Central Asian countries, and beyond it to the Roman Empire and the Mediterranean. There was some trade to East Africa also. Science, especially astronomy, mathematics, medicine and chemistry also registered a growth during this period. Painting, sculpture, literature and architecture also reached a high level, so that the period between the 4th and 6th centuries A.D. in North India, and 8th to 10th centuries in South India are considered classical ages.

The period between the 6th and 10th centuries in North India is considered a period of crisis and decline although there is controversy regarding its causes and nature. There was apparently a slowing down in economic activity in North India: many old towns declined, as also long distance trade, so that many trade guilds (*shrenis*) engaged in this trade suffered an eclipse, or were reduced to the status of caste groups. There seems to have been a growing rigidity of the mind, especially in arts and philosophy. The

Khwarizmi savant, al Biruni, who spent twelve years in India towards the end of the 10th and the beginning of the 11th century noted:

> "They (the Hindus) are by nature niggardly in communicating that which they know, and they take the greatest possible care to withhold it from men of another caste among their own people."

He goes on to say:

> "According to their belief, there is no other country on earth but theirs, no other race of men but theirs, and no created being besides them have any knowledge of science whatsoever."

And he concludes sadly:

> "... Their ancestors were not as narrow-minded as the present generation is."

The theory that the decline of long distance trade was attributable to the rise of Islam in West Asia is no longer accepted by Indian scholars. On the other hand, there is evidence to show that there were many contacts between the Abbasid court at Baghdad and Indian doctors, savants, merchants and even master-craftsmen. However, the nature of the Indo-Arab contacts and their impact on India still needs to be worked out.

Continuation of India's overseas trade with the Arab world, and the visit of Arab travellers and preachers to South India and the Western sea-coast are well known. Although Sind was conquered by the Arabs in the 7th century and Punjab was brought under the sway of the Persianized Turkish rulers of Ghazna towards the beginning of the 11th century, the real impact of Islam in India began only with the Turkish conquest of North India towards the end of the 12th and the beginning of the 13th century.

II

The Turkish conquest of India was more than a political conquest. It coincided with a deep-seated crisis in Indian society and culture, and resulted in far-reaching changes in religious ritual and belief, structure of society and, in some cases, even attitudes and values. A cultural efflorescence in the field of architecture, music, paintings and even literature which attained a climax during the 17th century under the great Mughals was a manifestation of this development. The extent to which this development is traceable to the direct contribution of the Turko-Afghan ruling classes and to what extent it may be attributed to the Indian response to an external crisis are matters of debate. What is more meaningful, however, is to pinpoint the factors which made possible a fruitful interaction between two civilizations which appeared so dissimilar and which had confronted each other for hundreds of years earlier.

It has been usual among scholars, especially Europeans, to emphasize the differences between the Indians and the Turkish invaders in social structure, religious ideas and even cultural values and attitudes. Thus, the Turkish tribal ideas and practices (emphasis on purity of blood, slavery); the Islamic ideas (monotheism, opposition to idol worship, belief in *jihad*); and cultural attitudes (simplicity, opposition to anthropomorphism, etc.) have been emphasized, and contrasted to Hindu ideas, practices and belief. But this does not enable us to apprehend the factors which made an interaction between the two possible, as also the complex nature of the outcome.

The processes of interaction between "Islam" and "Hinduism" can, for purposes of analysis, be posited at three different levels:

(i) At the political level, including the State formation.

(ii) At the level of the masses, involving religious movements and economic developments.

(iii) At the intellectual and cultural level, involving the middle sections and professionals.

These aspects or levels were obviously interconnected, and it would be dangerous to see them in isolation. We shall, therefore, cross from one to the other wherever considered desirable.

STATE FORMATION

Right from the time of the Arab conquest of Sind, but reaffirmed in the light of the situation prevailing in the Gangetic valley and adjoining areas, three ideas or assumptions formed the basis of the State in India, viz.:

(a) That it was not possible to effect large-scale conversion to Islam freely or by economic pressure and inducements. Hence, many non-Muslim features would have to be accepted, even if it meant disregarding the *sharia*. It also implied a tacit acceptance of the right of the Sultans to frame secular laws (*zawabit*), bearing in mind the political situation;

(b) Treating the Hindus as *ahl-i-kitab*, like the Jews or Christians, despite their being idol-worshippers, and granting them the status of *zimmis* and the freedom of worship with the restrictions it implied.

(c) Accepting the property rights of the Hindu cultivators and those holding superior rights in land even in territories under direct Turkish rule, i.e. those not held by Hindu Rajas. The Hindu Rajas also could be allowed to rule if they accepted the suzerainty of the Turkish ruler, permitted the practice of Islam in their territories, paid tribute etc. The debate, often fierce, regarding the character of the State which continued through out the Sultanate period as also under Mughal rule was, therefore, somewhat unreal. The

14th century historian, Ziauddin Barani, was right in saying that a truly Islamic State, based on *dindari* was not possible in India, but only one based on *jahandari* wherein open violation of the injunctions of the *sharia* was not permitted, but the basic concept of sharing power with the infidels was upheld. A further step in this direction was taken under Akbar in the 16th century. Hindu Rajas and zamindars were drawn actively in the armed forces and in the central administrative structure, and given officials ranks (*mansabs*). Although objected to by some orthodox thinkers, such as Baqi Billah, Shaikh Ahmed Sirhindi and a number of orthodox clergymen, this policy was continued by Akbar's successors, and was not reversed even by Aurangzeb who wanted to follow strictly the injunctions of the *sharia*.

The concept that the State in India had to be based on a sharing of power between the Hindus and the Muslims, or rather between the traditional Hindu landed ruling classes and the Muslims also found a reflection in the concept of *adl* or justice. According to popular notions, a just ruler dispensed equal justice to all irrespective of their faiths. Thus, the 14th century Sufi saint and poet Mulla Daud, praises the ruler of the times, Sultan Firoz Tughlaq (often portrayed as an orthodox, even bigoted ruler) for "treating the Hindus and the Turks (Muslims) alike."

MASS, POPULAR OR LOWER CLASS MOVEMENTS

By their very nature, these movements are the most difficult to document and study. Two aspects may be noted here:

(a) There was a steady increase in the number of Muslims, partly by migration from outside in the wake of Turkish conquest, large scale disruptions following the Mongol conquest of Central and Western Asia, and Afghan tribal movements during the 15th century. Second, on account of conversions, especially in the Sind and Punjab areas, as also in the urban areas being due in part to administrative exigencies and due in part to the influence of Sufi saints. The role of new professions, such as metallurgy, or paper-making, or expansion of weaving in conversions has yet to be studied.

(b) The rise of the Turkish state had both a direct and an indirect impact on the process of Hindu-Muslim rapprochement. An indirect effect was that it shattered the alliance of the Rajputs and the brahmans which dominated the scene in the previous four centuries and sternly suppressed any heterodox movements which challenged their supremacy, as also the religion of works favoured by the brahmans which sanctioned and legitimized inequality and discrimination based on caste. Destruction of temples and idols by the Turks hurt popular sentiments, but also tended to weaken the position of the brahmans, and their hold on the masses.

In a more direct manner, the concept of sharing of power, howsoever, hedged in and restricted by the ulema, created conditions for a greater interplay between the Hindus and Muslims. This process was speeded up under the Mughals when Rajputs, Kayasthas, and later the Marathas were given a share in power, i.e, in the army and the administrative structure. The mystical movements—the Sufi and Bhakti movements—which became mass, popular movements also played a positive role in the interaction between the Hindus and Muslims. Thus, Aurangzeb rejected the theory that a Muslim State had to base itself on the support of the Muslims alone, pointing to the urgent need of keeping the support of the Hindu rajas.

The Sufi movement had grown in West and Central Asia during the 8th-9th centuries, partially as a protest against growing materialism and inequality in Muslim society. In India some of the popular Sufi order, especially the Chishtiya, tried to keep aloof from the state, and its leading saints led a life of poverty, simplicity and resignation. They emphasized the mystical bond between God and his devotees, underlining the benign aspect of God, especially his love and compassion for the created beings. Their doors were open to the followers of all religions. The Sufi hospices (*khanqah*) which multiplied became a resort of the Yogis and the poor. In the Chishti *khanqahs*, Hindi bhakti poems continued to be used, though orthodox elements looked askance at it.

The ideas of a mystical bond with God through love and salvation have been traced back in India to the early centuries of the Christian era, and were broadcast widely in South India between the 6th and 10th centuries. The bhakti movement in North India which became widespread from the 14th century was influenced by the earlier movement and also imbibed some elements of Sufism. Thus, the idea of monotheism or unity of God-head, of the bond of love (rather than service) between God and his subjects, the idea of equality among believers etc. were emphasized. Some thinkers—Kabir, Nanak, Dadu, etc.—even denounced idol worship, the role of the clergymen as mediators with God, the caste system, etc. What is important for our purposes is not to try and ascertain to what extent these movements were successful in effecting changes in the structure of society, but the extent to which they were able to create a consciousness of defects and shortcomings in the social structure, and to create an intellectual and social ferment in which new ideas and institutions—even those associated with the "unclean foreigners" (*mlechcha*)—could be taken into account.

These developments were in large measure conditioned and promoted by economic, social and political developments. Of importance is the growth of a centralized state introduced by the Turks. This state depended upon the centralization of a high proportion of the agricultural surplus through the institution of the *iqtadari* or the *jagirdari* system, and the maintenance of a large standing army which was distributed in strategically-placed towns and cantonments., The growth of towns as centers of administration, trade and handicrafts between the 14th and 17th centuries had far reaching social and cultural implications. It has been noted that during the 17th century, there were three or four towns in North India which equalled in size the largest town in Western Europe, London and Paris. As is well known, everywhere in the world, towns have been a melting pot for peoples and ideas. New crafts were established, and older ones revived and strengthened to cope with the demands of the growing concourse of townsmen. Thus, metallurgy for the iron stirrups and later for artillery, paper industry, the spinning wheel and improved loom, extension of the water wheel (the *arrada*, often called in English the Persian water-wheel), were some of the new crafts introduced during early medieval period. Improved cement and building forms was an important factor in the growth of a new, magnificent form of architecture. Growth of towns and the strengthening of both internal and foreign trade partly due to improved communications with the Islamic world led to the growth and extension of the mercantile community. The growing unification of the country under the Mughals and the rapid growth of a money economy gave a further impetus to these trends. It is clear that the caste structure in India, considered by some 18th and 19th century English observers as the biggest factors inhibiting social mobility, had only a limited impact on economic and cultural growth during the medieval period. Caste groupings among the workers were not so rigid as to prevent them from taking to new professions. In such cases, the new professions gave birth to new caste groups. Thus, workers in glass (*sisgar*), makers of paper (*kagadi*), makers in lac (*lakhera*) mentioned by a 17th century literary work among thirty-six castes of artisans appear to be new. It is interesting to note that in some of the new crafts a majority of the workers were Muslims. However, in some of the professions, there was a good deal of sharing and give and take.

It is clear that by the 16th century, the social and intellectual rigidity noted by al-Biruni in the 11th century had been replaced by vigorous intellectual and cultural activity. The growth of magnificent buildings at Delhi, Agra, Lahore, etc., the growth of music and painting, and of secular literary forms in Indian languages using similar and sometimes literary forms (*qasida*, *ghazal*, *sher*, etc.) from Persian, the development of Urdu in the 18th century, all testified to a new cultural form which has been called Indo-Mughal. In the economic field, development was speeded up by the introduction of new fruits, and the improvement of old ones by the technique of grafting, and by spreading new products such as tobacco, maize, potato, etc., introduced into India by the Protuguese. This and the expansion of cash crops such as cotton, indigo, oilseeds, sugarcane, tobacco, etc. tended to break the isolation of the villages and link them more closely with the national market.

INTELLECTUAL MOVEMENTS

In the intellectual sphere too, a new elite group makes its appearance. This group which should be demarcated from the traditional Hindu elite, the brahmans, and the Mughal elite—the nobility and the official clergy, was as yet nebulous. In this new emerging group one could include the Kayasthas, i.e, the Hindus who had adopted Persian and found jobs in the government bureaucracy, and the professionals such as doctors (*hakims*), lawyers, etc., gentlemen of leisure, i.e, those who lived on income from orchards, markets and shops (*katra*), etc. as also a set of bankers (shroffs) and businessmen—especially Kashmiris and Khatris who had close links with the Mughal ruling class. It was this group rather than the traditional elite which took the lead during the 18th century in popularizing Urdu, a composite language based on Hindi and Persian. However, Persian remained the official language. Rapprochement, it may be noted, did not mean the extinction of the identity of the Muslims. According to the Indian tradition, each group (caste, religion, tribe) not only had the right but was expected to maintain its distinctive way of life, while accepting certain common principles. The Muslims continued to maintain a distinctive set of values and beliefs which provided a basis for the feeling of their being a distinct community (*qaum*). At the same time, social and linguistic groups drawn from members of different faiths interacted and often found common points of action.

By the 17th century, it was apparent to many European observers that India lagged behind Europe in the fields of science and technology. This lag which had started earlier, widened further during the 18th century with serious consequences for India, as also for many countries in Asia and Africa. This was part of a wider problem, the problem of the older civilizations in Asia and North Africa lagging behind European sciences and technology. A satisfactory answer to this growing divide can be given only by a closer cooperation between the scholars belonging to these countries. Even in our present state of knowledge, it can, however, be asserted that the European tendency to push back the relative stagnation of Islamic and Asian sciences and technology as far back in time as possible, i.e, to the fall of the Abbasides, in the 10th-11th centuries, does not have any substantial basis. Needham postulated the idea that whereas science and technology could travel from east to the west, there was a barrier across Syria and Iraq to its filtration from west to the east. This thesis, howsoever eminent its origin, can scarcely be accepted. In the case of

India, we have already referred to the rapid absorption of "foreign" agricultural products such as maize, tobacco, etc. in India. There was definite growth in the field of metallurgy and artillery in India during the 17th century, as also shipbuilding. Flint guns were widely used by the Afghan infantry during the 18th century to defeat the Marathas. However, this absorption of technology was not backed up by the development of basic sciences. The reasons for this, it would appear, were two-fold. First, religion and the popular saints, both Sufi and Bhakti, who had helped earlier to loosen the rigid bonds of society, and in effecting a rapprochement between the Hindus and the Muslims, had themselves become narrow and dogmatic. Their entire approach was anti-rational and not conducive to the growth of the secular sciences. This, and clerical opposition, were important factors in defeating efforts made by a liberal-minded monarch such as Akbar to introduce a new system of education in which mathematics and secular sciences would be made compulsory subjects of study. Similarly, interest in mechanical sciences and devices such as a machine for cleaning multiple gun barrels, multi-barreled cannon, a mobile gun-carriage, a wagon-mill for grinding corn, etc. introduced during Akbar's time, made no progress, and died.

In the ultimate resort, it would appear that like the Hindu elite of the 10th and 11th centuries, the Mughal elite also had become insular and haughty. The French traveler, Bernier, mentions the interest of some nobles in the government and even philosophical ideas prevalent in Europe at the time. But none in their science or naval technology. Many European travellers and agents of European governments travelled to India from the 16th century onwards. But no Indian travellers or savants thought it fit to travel to Europe. The brilliance of the Mughals dazzled the minds of contemporaries, while society and thought became more and more static and moribund.

The very meticulousness of the Mughal organizational structure became a barrier in the path of development, leading to a breakdown. The highly centralized militaristic state structure of the Mughals, where a military rank (*mansab*) determined the status of a noble, and the domination of the countryside by a military-minded landed gentry (the *zamindars*) with whom the Mughals had a working alliance, left little scope for the trader or the master-craftsman, or the more enterprising cultivator to assert themselves, as happened in the west. Centralization, though based on a basically feudal social order, had at the outset, helped in the process of economic growth. It could no longer subserve it, or take it to a higher stage.

III

The collapse of the Mughal empire in the 18th century was a part of a wider phenomenon in which highly centralized 'feudal' empires, such as the Safwid, the Ottoman and the Chinese collapsed one after another, providing an opportunity which was skillfully utilized by European powers, especially the English and the French, which were at a higher stage of scientific and technological development. The social, economic, political and organizational processes of the "colonial era," and its impact on the subject peoples has been a matter of considerable controversy. At the outset, it may be stated that the 18th century in India was not a period of "anarchy"—of breakdown of law and order and all kind of social norms, as has been argued by some British historians of the 18th and 19th centuries. During the first half of the 18th century, the all-India Mughal empire was replaced by a series of regional states based on an emerging balance of power—a phenomenon not unusual in Indian history, the main players being regional states of comparable size. Could any of these successor states have displayed a greater willingness or ability than the Mughals to adopt or absorb European science and technology, or some of their organizational methods in the field of commerce? This was not an impossibility, as may be demonstrated by two examples. The first was the case of Tipu Sultan of Mysore, who, in conjunction with the French, tried to open modern manufactories, especially in artillery, and to encourage trade by establishing joint stock companies, modern navigation and secular education. But he was defeated by the British before he could make much headway. The second was the example of the Sikhs in the Punjab. Drawn largely from the upper agricultural and artisan castes, the Sikhs in the Punjab traditionally had a more open society and a greater degree of internal mobility than Hindu or even Muslim society. During the first half of the 19th century, the Sikhs were able to develop a military organization and a modern artillery which, for the first time, could match the British in the two Anglo-Sikh wars (1840, 1842). Recent studies show that the guns were manufactured in the Punjab with the help of imported steel, the manufactories having been developed during the first half of the 19th century.

At a more fundamental level, efforts to reform Indian society, and to introduce modern science and technology, as well as the western system of education and rationalism into India began in the eastern parts of India, in Bengal, during the first half of the 19th century. The name of Raja Ram Mohan Roy, and his band of supporters—Dwarkanath Tagore, Keshab Chandra Sen, etc.—may be mentioned in this context. There has been controversy regarding the actual achievements of this early band of reformers, especially their tendency of appealing to the British for support in social reforms, such as banning immolation of widows (*sati*), female infanticide, etc. But it has been widely noted that their stand was the starting-point of the struggle for social reforms in the face of bitter opposition by the orthodox elements. Also, Ram Mohan Roy did underline the authoritarian nature of British rule in India, the gap between their democratic pretension and actions, and its harmful consequences. He thus also foreshadowed the struggle for democracy which was later taken up by the national leaders in India.

During the 19th century, we see at work two different types of responses to the shock of British conquest, and the challenge posed by Western science and technology and by the western Christian missionary for whom everything native was "barbaric superstition" or "heathenish ignorance." One type of response may be broadly described as "revivalist" in the sense that it wanted to purge society of the dross created by feudal inegalitarianism and sensualism by returning to an ideal society posited in the past and authenticated by religious or scriptural sanction. The movements of Shah Waliullah and of Abdullah Barelavi who later sought inspiration from the Wahabi movement fall into this category, as also the Arya Samaj movement founded by Dayanad Saraswati and the Ramakrishna movement whose leading light was Vivekanand. The differences in the approach, and the development of each of these movements in the overall historical perspective is not pertinent for us here. Their basic approach was to assert the authenticity of the native culture and tradition which was under attack, while simultaneously rejecting western science and rationalism as alien, and as being subversive of the moral order as perceived by them. Hence, they rejected simultaneously western education, and serving the western masters—the two being closely identified.

The second type of response was represented by Ram Mohan Roy, who though himself a product of traditional Sanskrit and Perso-Arab educational systems, advocated western education as means of mastering western science and technology, considered to be the basis of British victories in India. Both sections rejected the Christian and the utilitarian-rationalist attack on Indian culture. Nor did they consider it feasible or desirable that the British be assimilated into Indian culture like the earlier conquerors because they were considered to be basically different, with their interests outside India which was not the case of earlier invaders.

The nineteenth century in India, for all its seeming placidity, was thus a period of intense debate and discussion which had a considerable bearing on the national movement and its attitudes and values. At first, the British rulers considered the "liberal rationalist" elements to be their natural allies. They adopted a number of measures designed to weaken the position of the orthodox sections. Thus, the dispossession of many traditional landlords (zamindars) who were patrons of the orthodox elements and the working of the Inam Commission which confiscated on a large scale properties granted by earlier rulers for religious and educational purposes are two such examples. The working of the English law courts also meant the steady displacement of the traditional elites, both rural and religious. *This was the background to many of the traditional elements who joined the uprising of 1857.* This uprising undoubtedly had a mass basis in large areas. Although the liberal educated sections in Bengal kept aloof from it, the uprising kindled a spark of patriotism which was difficult to suppress. The British drew from this the lesson that they should, in future, support "the natural leaders of the people," viz. the landed elements who, in turn, were the allies of those who favoured the *status quo*. But at another level, the second half of the nineteenth century marked the beginning of the railway age in India. While this dealt a further blow to Indian handicrafts and opened up the heartland for the penetration of the British manufacturers and the export of raw materials from India, it prepared the ground, as Marx had postulated, for the growth of forces in India which would dig the grave of British rule in India.

The failure of the traditional elements to oust the British and the steady development of the new social classes, the "middle classes," as well as a working class led to changes in attitudes and approaches. Further, the defeat of the "mutineers" was considered the victory once again of British science and technology (the telegraph, the railways, the steamship, etc.) and organization. It is significant that the first three Universities in India, Calcutta, Bombay and Madras, were sanctioned in 1856, two years after the first Indian textile mill had been set up in Bombay. However, hopes of a rapid development of Indian industry, growth of science and technology, and expansion of job opportunities were belied by subsequent developments.

The second half of the nineteenth century saw the birth of an organized national movement in the country, under the leadership of the Indian National Congress (1885). A limited body at first, largely confined to small English-educated sections, it soon realized that none of their ambitions could be attained without bringing the masses into the movement. This immediately posed a dilemma. The masses had their own economic and social demands which did not always coincide with the interests of the English-educated sections, many of which were drawn from groups which were small or medium landlords. Moreover, the masses were still deeply traditional and under the influence of big landlords and their allies, the traditional religious leaders.

The last decade of the nineteenth and the first half of the twentieth century saw the gradual forging of links between the liberal educated classes and the mass of the people, especially the peasants and the artisans. Obviously, there were many diverse views in the matter, with consequently different programmes of action. At first, the leaders of the Congress had fought shy of getting involved in religious issues or putting forward proposals for social reforms, however desirable that may be, from *the platform of the National Congress,* lest it lead to divisions both within and between communities. But it was soon realized that it was not only difficult to maintain such a distinction in practice; it also left the field free for religious leaders whose vision of India was based on traditional values, not on science and technology and western education. A most thorough-going re-appraisal in the matter was carried out by Gandhi. He included in his political programme a programme of social reform and national regeneration. The demand for "representative government" was revised to "dominion status" and then to "independence" (1931). The weaker sections were to be brought up by the abolition of untouchability (which he called a "sin") and reviving rural handicrafts through support of *swadeshi* or indigenous products. Rural reconstruction, fair rents, and fixity of tenure were designed to appeal to the peasants. Women were to be brought on par with men through education, abolition of *purdah* (the veil) and the practices which stood in the way of their growth, e.g. child marriage, ban on widow remarriage, especially among middle class Hindus, etc. English was to be replaced by modern Indian languages and dignity of work emphasized, for which purpose the educational system was to be recast. People were to be brought nearer to administration by reviving the traditional village assemblies, the *pachayats.*

This programme, which helped to raise the aspirations of the people, had a number of limitations and was criticized by a section of the liberals as also by a section of the entrepreneurs and subsequently by sections, we may broadly designate "socialist." The liberals were dismayed at Gandhi's suspicion of and reservations about modern science and technology, his reservations about western education and his use of religious parables and terms to broadcast and defend his programme, so much so that he quickly acquired the mantle of a Hindu religious saint, the Mahatma. It was perhaps not fully realized by these sections that Gandhi was throwing a challenge to the traditionalist religious leaders as also building a bridge with them. They could hardly reject his concept of social reform, since they themselves were critical of the existing reality. As a perceptive modern sociologist, A.R. Desai, observes, "On the whole, national progress became the main objective of these reconstructed religions" even though they talked in terms of reviving a mythical past.

More serious was the feeling that Gandhi did not favour modern industry and talked vaguely of a peasant egalitarian utopia, the Ram Rajya. As the socialists, which included Jawaharlal Nehru, pointed out, the ills of capitalism which led to the exploitation of the weaker sections and an acquisitive outlook, had to be separated from modern science and technology which were the *sine qua non* of a modern nation. Thus, the old 19th century debate resurfaced, but in a different form. Nor was the debate pursued to a point where it might endanger the unity of the national struggle for freedom. Even though the Communists left the Congress in 1945, largely on issues of tactics, they largely continued to support the Congress and the struggle for freedom.

The withdrawal of the British power from India in 1947 after setting up two countries, India and Pakistan, is a fact of history and need not concern us here. Despite agreeing to the Muslim majority areas of the North-West and East Bengal being constituted into a separate State, on the basis of religion, the Indian leaders rejected the idea that religion could be the basis of a national or nation state. India upheld the concept of "a secular, democratic republic" with equal rights to all, irrespective of sex, creed, caste or religion. However, this was more an aspiration than a reality.

IV

The attainment of state power faced the leaders with the twin tasks of redeeming the promises made by them to the Indian people and, simultaneously, to define their goals, ambitions and priorities more clearly than they had done during the struggle against the Colonial power. The concept of a democratic state based on the concept of secularism and freedom of expression, assembly, etc. was sought to be enshrined in the Indian Constitution which was based on adult franchise—itself a revolutionary concept in the Indian context. This was followed by the re-organization of the States on a linguistic basis—a process which is still not completed. The Hindu Code Bill (1955-56) passed in the teeth of orthodox opposition sought to grant the Hindu women a status of equality with men. Steps were also taken to revive and foster Indian culture in the fields of dance, music, painting, and fine arts, handicrafts, drama, etc.

One of the most important steps taken at the outset was the setting up of the Planning Commission (1950) for preparing a blueprint for India developing into a modern industrialized state as quickly as possible. This was a continuation of the Planning Board set up by the Congress in 1936 under the chairmanship of Jawaharlal Nehru for speeding up the industrial development of the country—a step taken, significantly enough when Gandhi was alive and at the helm of the Congress and whose concept based of Hind Swaraj was a kind of a decentralized polity based on the village. A second major decision was to set up the Council of Scientific and Industrial Research with a chain of National Science Laboratories which would help indigenous development of technology. National objectives in this field were spelt out for the first time in the Science Policy document (1958), which had received the personal attention of Nehru.

The rapid development of India's industrial infrastructure and agriculture during the comparatively brief span of fifteen years from 1950 to 1965 gave the quietus to many nineteenth century stereotypes sedulously fostered by western imperialists to mask their anti-people and anti-development policies, such as "the unchanging Orient," "India being a slave to caste" (Max Weber), etc. A number of questions, however, arose. First, what was the relationship between development on the one hand, and participatory democracy and social justice on the other? Also, if India did succeed in building a modern industrial society, to what extent would it be able to maintain its cultural specificity?

In a broad sense, some of the socio-cultural constraints on faster economic development in India were caste, communalism, regionalism, a low scientific and technological development of the people, etc. Caste has been regarded as a specific feature of Indian civilization and culture, and a major factor in restricting internal mobility necessary for faster economic development. Despite a long tradition of scholarly study, the evolution and the working of the caste system in India is still imperfectly understood. Recent research suggests, however, that it was not as rigid as it was often presented to be. It both influenced and was influenced by secular developments, such as acquisition or loss of wealth and position, especially control over land, as we have noted earlier. Nor did hereditary profession of the crafts inhibit the development of new crafts in medieval times or new industry in modern times. It is this very adaptability which has made caste one of the most enduring social institutions in the world. Two divergent trends in relation to caste seem to be at work in modern India. Social intercourse between people belonging to the same profession or enjoying similar social prestige, emoluments, etc. has increased. But marriages are still largely arranged and take place, in the main, within the same caste. Caste and family ties reinforce each other and act as a channel for transmitting traditional values and attitudes. To what extent the influence of caste and family have weakened, especially in the cities, largely on account of education and the powerful influence of cinema, television, etc. in projecting a common culture is an open-ended question, especially on account of the influx of large numbers of people from rural areas having traditional values.

Surprisingly, the caste sentiment has been reinforced by the working of the system of parliamentary democracy, and elections to civic bodies at various levels from the Centre, State and the village. Choice of candidates to these bodies is often made bearing in mind the electoral strength of various castes (and communities) in various constituencies. Growing influence of caste at the political level will, it is feared, have a deleterious effect on efficiency. The question of reverse discrimination versus merit has become a political question.

Developmental theories in the West have undergone a great deal of change in recent years. The "modernization" theory, which assumed that a number of developing countries would, under western aegies, speedily discard their traditional forms and institutions in favour of western ones and that this would lead to the establishment of a modern industrial society has been replaced by the "centre-periphery" theory which implies that given the present international division of labour as also of scientific talent and resources, the newly developing countries can develop only in a limited manner, i.e. as satellites or virtual dependencies of the developed "centre." In this context, attention has been shifted to the social and cultural constraints on development and to the "hetrogenetic villages" which are the inheritors of tradition but not susceptible to speedy change, the dichotomy between the "great culture" and the "little culture," etc. However, the Indian experience shows that there is no necessary contradiction between the maintenance of traditional national cultural forms and industrialization, and that many traditional social institutions and values are not opposed to economic development. The speed with which peasants in many parts of India took to modern farming techniques once their success had been demonstrated, thus creating what has been called the Green Revolution without, however, giving up their traditional social forms is a case in point. However, such a development would not have been possible in the absence of an industrial infrastructure.

The role of education, and of developing a cadre of scientists and technologists who can serve at high as well as intermediate levels, is also indisputable. Experience in India shows that it is easier to train high-grade scientists than middle-level technicians for the latter cannot be done without raising and restructuring the inherited educational system as also the inherited values of assigning a lower place in society to one who works with his hands. Also, while education is the single most important vehicle of vertical mobility, and has led to multiplication of demand for higher education by rich and medium farmers, education by itself cannot change the social system or usher in an egalitarian society without necessary developments at the political and economic level so.

Certain entrepreneurial and liberal sections in India now concede that the infrastructure of industry could not have been built up in India without governmental interference in a big way and the planning process. But they argue that this fundamental job having been done, the planning system and with it the public sector should take a back seat and let the market forces to operate. A variation of this theme is that faster development would take place if Government were to give priority to agriculture with full backing to those who can deliver the goods, i.e. the rich and medium farmer.

The rise of the rich and middle class farmers has led to many problems and new tensions, such as the growing tension between these sections and the landless, predominantly scheduled caste elements who are denied the right of ownership of land. The rise of regional parties to power and their greater assertiveness in economic and other spheres is also to a considerable extent backed by these classes. The central liberal elite which led the national movement and which strongly favoured a parliamentary system and a secular polity, therefore, finds itself challenged from various quarters. The rise of money power, especially of black money, has also, to some extent, eroded its public image. Simultaneously, those socialist elements which had hoped that a large public sector would pave the way for socialism and a classless society are deeply disappointed. Youth is restive on account of slow development leading to widespread unemployment, both among the educated and the uneducated or the less well educated.

India is thus beset with serious problems, but these are basically problems of growth. What is being demanded is faster and more balanced growth, *not* that modern science and industry is inimical to Indian culture or to its value system. Thus, India has come a long way since the turn of the century. The traditions of the national movement are still a vital sustaining force. There is a consensus that the unity of India is the necessary basis for development. The growth of mass and higher education,* economic development, communications and popular cultural forms (films, TV, etc.) are broadening the central elite, and strengthening the bonds of national unity.

Despite the seriousness of the challenge, India is poised for a faster rate of growth, based on its increased capacity for

*There were almost 3 million students on roll in Universities and colleges in 1981-82 with an annual out turn of 25, 000 engineers and 50,000 trainees of polytechnics.

absorption of sophisticated technology, and by linking its large scientific manpower more closely with productivity, reviewing and updating its educational structure as well as its administrative and managerial system. India cannot afford to lose the battle for self-reliant development based on social justice, democracy, secularism and pride in its hoary past, and seems well set to win. However, it will have to travel an arduous and exacting trail in order to attain its goal.

CHAPTER VI

Historical Relations between India and Turan 15th-18th Centuries

Babur has rightly been called the link between India and Central Asia. Although Turks from Ghaur had conquered India towards the end of the 12th century, and Turkish sultans ruled over large parts of India for the next two centuries, there was no real link between the Indian Turks and the Turks of Central Asia because with the rise of the Mongols, meaningful ties between India and Central Asia had been virtually snapped. This was not the case with the Mughals, or more correctly, the Chughtai Turks. Babur, the first Mughal ruler in India, always had the ambition of conquering Samarqand, the capital of his ancestor, Timur, which was also a cultural magnet for entire central Asia. In fact, the relationship of India with Central Asia revolved around the triangle formed by the cities of Samarqand, Bokhara and Balkh, with Samarqand constituting the political and cultural center, Bokhara the spiritual centre, and Balkh the centre for trade and commerce. Babur did not succeed in keeping Samarqand under his control for any length of time. But what he learnt at Samarqand he tried to put into practice in India later on.

The influence of Central Asia, exercised through Babur, may be seen, first and foremost, in the emergence of a new concept of the state—the Turko-Mongol theory of sovereignty. The Turks, the Iranians and the Mughals considered the position of a sovereign as something more than simply that of a leader. In an era marked by clan and feudal disintegration, it was felt that only a leader imbued with a sense of love for the people would be able to provide justice and stability. The position of the leader or the Sultan was sought to be buttressed by ascribing supernatural qualities to him. Thus, Chingiz was considered to be the Son of Light. Apart from meeting the challenge from clan and feudal elements, the Sultan had to deal with the demands of the clergy for special privileges, as also their claims to determine right and wrong, as also to shape the policy of the state according to their lights. Timur believed that since God is one and has no partner, therefore, the vice- regent (the King) over the land of the Lord must be one. Accordingly he lays down that the King must make the people feel that he is not under the influence of anybody (*Malfuzat-i-Taimuri*). This did not mean that he advocated unrestrained use of power. He himself showed considerable regard for his nobles and officials. But the final decision had to rest with the sovereign, who might or might not follow the counsels of his officials.

This was in essence the policy advocated by Akbar when, shortly after assuming the personal direction of the affairs of the state, he abolished the poll-tax (*jizyah*) on non-Muslims in 1562, and also discontinued the practice of the forcible conversion of prisoners of war. Later, he entered into matrimonial relations with the Rajput rajas– traditional rulers who traced their descent from the Sun and the Moon! This was a conscious co-mingling of two traditions, and strengthening the legitimacy of the Mughal ruler.

To further assert his independence of the clerical elements, Akbar revived the ancient Central Asian concept that royalty was a light emanating from God, and a ray from the Sun "without the intermediate assistance of anyone." (*Ain-i-Akbari*).

The idea of an essentially secular state in which "sectarian differences do not raise the dust of strife," was combined with the idea of a state which was a leader in the field of culture. The *Yasa-i-Chingizi* or *Taura-i-Chaghtai* to which Babur and Akbar refer repeatedly, was, above all, a code of conduct for persons in authority.

The cultural sensibility inculcated by the *Taura* was reflected also in various cultural fields, including the setting up of numerous gardens by Babur, both at Kabul and in Hindustan. These gardens emphasized order, regularity, communion with nature, and a sense of spiritual peace, and must be regarded as one of the gifts of Central Asia to India. The practice of laying out gardens was copied on a large scale by the nobles. Through them, many trees and shrubs, flowers as well as fruit-trees, traveled from Central Asia to India, and perhaps in the reverse direction as well. Although these are not discussed in contemporary sources, a careful study of the paintings of the period could throw some useful light on the subject. The various types of melons imported into India from the time of Babur were sought to be acclimatized in India. The *Ain* speaks of the horticulturists of Iran and Turan having settled in India to improve the cultivation of trees. Thus, exchange of technology between Iran and Turan was practiced in those days—something which was interrupted with the colonial domination of India. Reference is made to the extension of cultivation of melons, water-melons, peaches, grapes, almonds, pistachios, pomegranate, etc., which, as a result, "are everywhere to be found." (*Ain*, I, p. 68). Improved variety of grapes was another, though the wine industry as such (as distinct from distillation and production of strong spirits called *arq*) seems not to have developed in India. The technique of grafting, which had begun earlier, seems to have developed further, perhaps as a result of interaction with Central Asian techniques. It led to the production of many new strains of mangoes. We know that many fruits from Central Asia were brought to the tables of the nobles, during the 16th and 17th centuries. Melons, pears and apples were imported even from Samarqand. Was there a trade of mangoes, and other typical Indian fruits in the reverse direction?

Thus, it may be said that there was, to a considerable extent, a shared sensibility during this period between the peoples of India and Central Asia regarding the need for social order and stability, and the nature of the state which was necessary for serving this, as also the real needs of the people. However, the experience of the peoples of India and Central Asia in further developing such a state was different. In India, the Mughals made considerable progress in building a highly centralized state in which people of different race, religions and communities were actively involved. But they were not able to defend the livelihood and other interests of the people. Hence, there was a phase of disintegration or colonial rule before a people's movement could recreate a state based on people of different religions, languages and ethnic elements. In Central Asia, the elements of tribal and feudal disunity could be overcome only on the basis of socialism.

The contest for Samarqand between Shaibani Khan and the Timurids had created barriers of mutual suspicion which dissolved with the consolidation of Mughal rule under Akbar, and the unification of Turan under Abdullah Khan. Akbar had little interest in recovering his ancestral homeland, Farghana, though he liked to dwell on it on occasions, largely for diplomatic reasons. Even at this period, India's foreign policy was essentially peace-loving, while maintaining close relations with Iran and Turan, as well with the Ottoman Turks, who were then the masters of Baghdad. Akbar skillfully avoided being drawn into the struggle between the Uzbeks and the Persians for the control of Khurasan including Herat.

Akbar refused to be drawn into an alliance against Persia in the name of struggle against Shi-ism. Nor was he prepared to join the Safvids against the Uzbeks in pursuit of the mirage of the Mughal homelands. Akbar's policy of neutrality, or non-alignment in modern parlance, yielded rich dividends. The Mughals were able to consolidate Afghanistan by entering into an accord with Abdullah Khan, the ruler of Turan, in 1686. In an exchange of letters with Abdullah Khan, Akbar accepted his suggestion of the Hindu Koh being the boundary between Afghanistan and Turan. Abdullah Khan also agreed to maintain neutrality in Mughal efforts to recover Qandahar from Iran, a task which Akbar accomplished in 1695, thus reintegrating the Afghans, In return, Akbar withdrew Mughal claims on Badakhshan.

In his letter to Abdullah Khan, Akbar also pointed to the rising danger from the activities of the Europeans in the Indian Ocean. Akbar sharply castigated the "Firangi infidels" who have "lifted the head of turbulence, and stretched out the hand of oppression" in the Indian Ocean. Although Akbar referred specifically to their interference with pilgrim traffic to Mecca, his indictment of the Portuguese extended to their policy of seeking a colonial domination of the Indian Ocean, with monopolization of specific items of trade, including horses which was a vital item of military defence in those days. India's contacts with the Ottomans—the most powerful Muslim state at the time, in an effort to counter the growing colonial domination of the Indian Ocean by the Portuguese is, however, an item for a separate discussion.

Friendly relations between India and Turan continued under Jahangir, so much so that when in 1622, the Iranians captured Qandahar from the Mughals, the Uzbek ruler, Imam Quli, dispatched Abdur Rahim Khwaja to the Mughal court, and offered cooperation in the projected campaign under Shah Jahan to recover it.

The brief hostilities between India and the Uzbek ruler, Nazar Muhammad, during the reign of Shah Jahan did not reflect any real change of policy by either side. It was really an off-shoot of the civil war, first between Nazar

Muhammad and his brother, Imam Quli, and then with his son, Abdul Aziz. Partition of the empire had been a Timurial legacy, often leading to civil war, or reckless adventure by one of the dissatisfied princess. The brief war cooled the hot-heads on both sides, and restored good relations which continued till the rise of Nadir Shah.

Friendly relations between India and Turan during this period facilitated movement of men and materials between the two, so much so that Abul Fazl, who considered India to be the leading country in the Islamic world, grudgingly admitted that under Abdullah Khan "Turan became somewhat civilized." (*Akbar Nama*, iii 737). A careful scrutiny of the items exchanged between India and Turan during the various diplomatic exchanges would be a fruitful item of study. Though our chroniclers often confine themselves to exchange of "varieties," or "noble presents," details are sometimes given. Thus, in 1586, Abdullah Khan sent through Mir Quraish, who belonged to the noble family of Saiyids, "Choice horses, strong camels, swift mules, animals of the chase, and choice *postins* (garments of fur) and other rarities of the country." Carpets must have been one of the rarities because the *Ain* refers to the *gilims* (carpets) of Iran and Turan as the standard, while claiming that Akbar had appointed experienced workmen whose products were a match to these. (*Ain*, Blochman, p. 57).

The movement of goods was matched by the movement of human beings from both sides. The role of the Iranis and Turanis in the service of the Mughals has been a frequent subject of comment, both for contemporary European travellers, as also for later Imperialist historians. Thus, the Frenchman, Bernier, considered the Mughal nobility as consisting of "foreign adventurers," mostly from Iran and Turan. Imperialist historians have compared the migrants from Iran and Turan to the British civil servants who played a vital role in the Imperialist exploitation of India. It was forgotten that unlike the British who had a power base outside India, and for whom India was always an "alien" country to be exploited, the bulk of the Irani and Turani migrants made India their home, assimilating themselves to Indian culture and enriching it with their own insights and skills.

Secondly, these observers did not generally take note of the constant exchange between India and Turan in the field of religion and thought. Khwaja Ubaidullah Ahrar, the founder of the Naqshabandi *silsilah*, was the patron saint of the Mughals, and the Naqshabandi order flourished in India on account of their patronage. Every Sufi saint in India had the ambition of traveling to Samarqand and Bokhara and Ajani in order to complete their spiritual training. The history and impact of these exchanges is another field which needs careful study.

The very fact that in the 18th century, Jai Singh, the ruler of Amber, drew on the *Zich-i-Ulugh Khani*, and tried to reproduce at Jaipur and Delhi, the observatory of Samarqand is testimony to the continued interaction between India and Turan in all fields, including the scientific, up to the 18th century, i.e, up to the period when the rise of Imperialism and the colonial subjection of India gradually sundered these historic ties.

CHAPTER VII

Central Asia—The New Great Game

The theory that the present struggle in Central Asia is virtually a repetition of the "great game" played in the nineteenth century between Britain and Russia, with USA taking the place of Britain needs serious modification. Not only are the orientations of the USA and Russia vastly different from their predecessors, the situation inside the Central Asian states is vastly different. These states are no longer the earlier feudal monarchies with narrowly based interests of the ruler and his cohorts. Also, the role of the neighbours, and "proximate neighbours," such as Turkey, Iran, India and China are important factors which have a serious bearing on the situation. Finally, while there is undoubtedly struggle for power and influence in the region between the United States and Russia, conflict between the two is no longer a dominant reality.

There is considerable discrepancy regarding the oil and gas resources in the Central Asian Republics (CARs), and there is keen rivalry regarding the pipelines for getting them out. Apart from financial and strategic considerations, the US wants access to Central Asian oil and gas to put pressure on OPEC, as was being done earlier with the help of North Sea oil which is now nearly exhausted.

Thus, the situation is a complex one and should not be judged merely in terms of historical precedents, because historical precedents are apt to be misleading. To project the situation in Central Asia largely in terms of a continuation of the nineteenth century struggle between Britain and Tsarist Russia is, in fact, a gross simplification of a complex situation.

Ahmed Rashid's book, *Taliban, Islam, Oil and the New Great Game in Central Asia* has become a subject of avid reading by diplomats, newspapermen and others, specially after 11 September, and the US attack on the Al-Qaeda network operating from Afghanistan and Pakistan, and aided by the Taliban. There are several assumptions behind the book which needs careful scrutiny. The first assumption is that there is an ongoing civilizational struggle between Islam and Christianity which was reflected in the struggle of Bosnia, and is an issue between the Jews and the Muslims in Palestine. The future of Islam in Central Asia is linked to the struggle between the Taliban and the USA which is considered the leader of the western world. It is, of course, accepted that solid material interests lie behind this civilizational struggle, just as the Crusades was also a struggle for the mastery of Lebanon which, during the times, was the primary centre of trade in oriental goods. Thus, the struggle for the mastery of the extensive oil and gas deposits and pipelines in the Central Asian Republics (CARs) is a part of the new great game.

The *second* basic assumption is that as in the 19th Century there is a struggle for the strategic space of Central Asia, with the USA replacing the British Imperialists, and Russia continuing to harbour the old Tsarist dream of a drive to the warm water ports through the help of Iran. Sometimes, China is also involved in this great game, largely because of its growing appetite for the oil and gas found in the region.

Before we examine these assumptions, some attention may be given to the question: what is meant by Central Asia, and what role has this region played in world history or strategic dispositions. Andre Gunder Frank, who has tried to study history as a world system and has written on "The Centrality of Central Asia," calls Central Asia as "a black hole in the astronomical sense ... it is also central to the civilizations of the outlying peoples, whose life space is sucked into the dark hole in the centre ... It is not clear where civilized peoples and space end, and where they interpenetrate with those of Central Asia." He goes on to say "Central Asia is also central to any attempt at systematic or systematic analysis of the world *system*."[1]

Khazanov[2] distinguishes Middle Asia from Inner or Central Asia. He limits Central/Inner Asia to Kashgaria, Junagaria (modern Sinkiang or Xinyiang), Mongolia and Tibet. The region bounded by the Caspian Sea in the west, the Aral Sea in the north, and the Hindukush and the Pamirs in the south and east he designates as Middle Asia. Some scholars argue that socio-politically speaking, Manchuria and even Korea were historically parts of Central/Inner Asia. Some others distinguish Central Asia and the neighbouring civilizations as between migratory and sedantary peoples, with the migratory area constantly shrinking, or being in a state of flux, climate having a great role in the process.

The point to note is that modern notions of ethnicity or nationalism are yet to develop in many parts of this area, and constant migrations have left a vast patchwork of peoples belonging to different races and languages. For practical purposes, political scientists consider Mongolia and Tibet as separate entities, applying the term Central Asia to the Muslim majority area comprising the Central Asian Republics and Sinkiang or Xinjiang. Afghanistan, especially the northern areas beyond the Hindukush inhabited by Uzbeks and Tajiks which had never been a part of Afghanistan till 1917, is sometimes also added to it.

Vast empires have swept across this area, and influenced the countries extending up to Eastern Europe as also India. The last such great empire was the Turkish empire of Timur whose descendent, Babur, established the Mughal empire in

[1]Frank, Andre Gunder. 1992. The Centrality of Central Asia, *Studies in History*, Vol. 8 (1), pp. 44-121.

[2]Khazanov, Anatoli M. 1979. *The Nomads and the Outside World*, C.U.P.

India. As rulers of Afghanistan, the Mughals kept close contact with Central Asia, especially with *Mawara-un-Nahar* or Transoxiana and its neighbour and rival, Iran. The Persian desire for Qandahar, and constant Uzbek incursions into Kabul forced the Mughals not only to maintain a high state of military alert in Afghanistan but to adopt diplomatic efforts to contain such incursions. The expedition of Shah Jahan to Balkh in 1642, with an accompanying force of Rajputs led by the Amber ruler, Jai Singh, was a military repost to this. I am mentioning this so that we do not consider the Indian involvement in Central Asia as just a British legacy.

It is hardly necessary to recall that Sir George Mackinder's theory of the struggle between the heartland and coastal areas, or between the core and the periphery, was first applied to Central Asia which he called "the geographical pivot of history." It was extended to Germany only later on.

The break up of the Soviet Union re-opened Central Asia to the world, and recent events in Afghanistan has made it a major focus of world affairs. It has been argued by the *Economist*[3] that the US's attitude towards the region is based primarily on strategic considerations, including Central Asian oil and gas, and that 11 September merely provided it an opportunity to establish itself firmly in the Central Asian states. The Russian attitude has been a guarded one: while agreeing to some of the Central Asian states notably Uzbekistan to allow the United States to station troops, air planes, and helicopters at an Uzbek air base and to use Uzbek territory to launch offensive air strikes on Afghanistan, and Russian troops joining the peace-keeping force in Afghanistan, Putin has made it clear that a long range American military presence in the region would not be welcome.

[3]*Economist*, 19 January, 2002, p. 29.

The trade-off between US desire for a military presence in the Central Asian Republics, long considered by Russia as its backyard, and the return of Russian troops to Kabul, an area from which its expulsion was considered by the US and the FBI as the high watermark in the Cold War, has to be seen in the framework of over-all US foreign policy and its relations with Russia and the neighbouring areas. In his pre-Presidential foreign policy presentation, George Bush had said, "In the breadth of its land, the talent and courage of its people, the wealth of its resources, and the reach of its weapons, Russia is a great power, and must always be treated as such...." Dwelling on the need of national security and threat of nuclear weapons, including from those he called "rogue states," and has now termed as "axis of evil," he said: "All this requires nothing short of a *new strategic relationship* to protect the peace of the world." (emphasis mine). Castigating the conduct of Chinese government as "alarming abroad and apalling at home," Bush, while prepared to deal with China, said "China is a competitor, not a strategic partner."[4]

In his most authoritative speech on foreign policy by George Bush in his "State of the Union" address to Congress in January, 2002, these passages do not occur. On the other hand, while proclaiming his desire to work with Russia, China and India to contain terrorism, he says that the US will not wait on events while dangers gather. The US "will not permit the world's most dangerous regimes to threaten us with the world's most destructive weapons." Thus, he takes a unilateral attitude on nuclear arms, virtually claiming the right to strike with nuclear arms for protection of American interests, thus setting at naught all treaties on control of nuclear weapons.[5]

[4]US Foreign Policy Agenda: Foreign Policy and the 2000 Presidential Election, US Embassy, New Delhi, pp. 31-24.

[5]Bidwai, Praful. 2002. *Hindustan Times*, 22 February.

As a counter to this, the idea of a Russia-China-India strategic triangle, first put forward by the Russian President, Gregory Primakov, at New Delhi in 1998, earlier considered little more than a theoretical proposition, has acquired a measure of diplomatic currency. However, much depends on the evolution of future US policy. As at present, each of the three parties, Russia, China and India is eager to establish closer economic and strategic relations with the USA while trying simultaneously to mend fences with each other.

The Central Asian "great game" has to be seen in this context. Just as the British and the Tsarist regime, while competing for political influence in Central Asia, patched up their differences when they perceived a greater danger from a militaristic Germany, the US and the Russians can adjust their differences on WMD, etc. if they perceive a greater danger or advantage to themselves.

In this scenario, two issues are important from India's point of view: first, the danger or prospects of rise or regrouping of *jihadi* forces in the region, and their possible involvement in Kashmir, and second, building enduring economic and cultural relations with the countries of the region, as also exploring the likelihood of getting cheaper oil and gas from them.

The main oil and gas deposits in CAR's are in Kazakhastan, Turkmenistan and Uzbekistan, whereas Kyrgyzstan and Tajikistan have enormous hydel resources. Estimates of oil and gas reserves in the CAR's vary. According to *Jane's Intelligence Review* (Vol. XII, No. 7, July 2000), the Caspian region holds 6,000 - 12,000 Mtos (4 to 7 per cent of global reserves). It may also hold 5,000 - 9,000 Mtos gas (5 to 8 per cent of global reserves). It concludes "Compared to the Middle East, where around 65 per cent of global reserves are to be found, Caspian reserves are therefore marginal." According to Edward L. Moore, Advisor at Hess Energy Trading Company, and James Richard, Portfolio Manager at Firebird Management, their reserves "are much larger than previously assumed." They add, "The one factor that constricts the ability of Russia and Kazakhastan to increase exports more than production capacity is infrastructure—namely, inadequate pipelines and port facilities."[6]

However, the earlier belief that by 2050, Central Asia would account for up to 80 per cent of US oil, appears to be wide off the mark.[7]

It is well known that one reason for the earlier sponsorship of the Taliban by the US was a desire to underwrite the Cent Gas Oil Consortium led by the Texan Oil Co., UNOCAL, and its project of laying a pipeline from Turkmenistan and Kazakhastan to a Gulf Sea port *via* Mazar-i-Sharif, Qandahar and Pakistan. China was also keen to lay down a pipelines across the Xinjiang (Sinkiang) region in view of the diminution of its earlier high expectations of oil from Xinjiang. The laying of these pipelines, it was accepted, would be enormously expensive, and its economic viability would remain in question as long as the prevailing low prices of oil persisted.

However, the questions of oil, gas, and pipelines have always been mired in politics. As has been pointed out by George Perry of the Brookings Institute, if the oil production or supply of oil from Saudi Arabia was to cause a drop of availability of a mere one million barrels per day, the price of oil would rise to $ 32 per barrel. If world availability was to be cut by 10 per cent, the price would zoom to $ 132 per barrel.[8]

[6]*Foreign Affairs*, The Battle for Energy Dominance, March-April, 2002, pp.16-31.

[7]Kalick, Jan. 2001. "Caspian Energy at the Cross Roads" in: *Foreign Affairs*, September-October, 2001; Chinoy, Anuradha M. Oil Plus Peace in Pipe Dream, *Asian Age*, 30 Nov. 2001.

[8]Quoted by Mohan Guruswamy, The Great Oil Game, *Asian Age*, 3 December, 2000.

Thus, access to Central Asian oil-fields would mean a balancing off of the OPEC. As Jan H. Kalick says in the *Foreign Affairs* (September-October, 2001), "oil and gas developments in the Caspian basin could help diversify, secure, and stabilize world energy supplies in the future, as resources from the North Sea has done in the past." As is well known, North Sea oil supplies are virtually exhausted. What is sought from the Central Asian or Caspian region is not to replace but to supplement, the Middle Eastern oil, and to some extent, to act as a pressure lever on the latter.

To what extent do US and Russian interests in CARs in oil and gas clash or coincide? In the capitalist world, both often go side by side. Thus, the Caspian Pipeline Consortium (CPC) is owned half by Russia, Kazakhastan and Oman, and eight companies including Chevron, Exxon Mobil and Luk Arco own the remaining half. Its pipeline exports oil from the Tenziz oil field through Russia to the Black Sea. Its planned capacity is 1.3 million barrels per day or more. Meanwhile, the B.P. led Azerbaijan International Operating Company (AIOC) is working with the Turkish state-owned pipeline company BOTAS on a multi-million dollar study of the Baku-Tbilisi-Ceyhan pipeline. However, attitudes are changing. The major Russian oil exporting firm Lukoil recently stated that it would even consider participating in the Baku-Ceyhan pipeline. Ceyhan is on Turkey's Mediterranean coast and would boost oil supplies to Europe, the United States and Turkey. This pipeline, expected to be completed by 2005, and was considered important as "Continued dependence on Russian pipelines would be dangerous because it would allow Moscow to unilaterally raise tariffs and constrain Caspian exports, or threaten these actions to win political or economic concessions from its neighbours."[9]

[9]Foreign Affairs, September-October, 2001, p.123

This, in a manner of speaking, reveals the US's own game in obtaining oil and gas concession in the CARs. It is not clear as yet which of these pipelines Bush would favour. However, denunciation of Iran as an "axis of evil" clearly signifies opposition to the proposed pipeline across Iran to Turkey, as also across to Bandar Abbas in which India has been interested.

While Russia may not any longer be in a position to pursue its old objective of access to the warm waters of the Indian Ocean, specifically to Persian Gulf ports, the new Central Asian states have clear interest in such access. Thus, they showed interest in joining the IOR-ARC, and put forward tentative claims as per UNCLOS agreement for land-locked states having access to the sea in agreement with littoral states. Iran itself has been keen to provide access to the Persian Gulf ports. However, the scheme for a new rail-cum-road link from Central Asia to the Iranian port, Shahbakar or Bandar Abbas, is still mired in controversy.

Central Asia has been called the cross-road of communication between China, Russia, India and the Mediterranean. Arnold Toynbee in his *Between Oxus and India* (CUP, 1961), had described Transoxiana as a place where "routes converged from all quarters of the compass and from which routes radiate to all quarters of the compass again." Maurice Lombard (*The Golden Age of Islam,* 1975) identified three related centres of particular importance to trans-Asian trade—Merv, Heart, Balkh and Nishapur on the road between Baghdad and India; Khwarazm in the Oxus delta was a pivot for both north-east, and north-south trade, and Transoxiana on the east-west road to China. For historic reasons, the Europeans emphasized only the road to China which, during the 19th Century the German Baron von Richtofen, wrongly called the "Silk Road" because silk was no longer the main item of export on that road. Nor was it the principal route of communication to the west, either in terms of the volume of the goods carried, or their value. The principal route of communication and trade with the west was undoubtedly the route to India *via* Qandahar, Multan or Kabul through which Indian textiles reached West and Central Asia and spices to the Mediterranean world (with the sea route *via* the Red Sea and Alexandria a second route). Efforts have been made in recent years to revive the old Asian trade routes, emphasis being given pride of place to the "silk road." But to be really effective, not only the east-west, but the north-south route to India need to be revived. Such a development can however take off only when relations between Pakistan and India improve. Such improvement is also important for CARs not only for trade, but for a pipeline across Afghanistan and Pakistan to India. According to some observers, economically this is the most viable. It would also cater to the growing energy needs of South and East Asian countries.

This brings us to the question of religious extremism. Here India faces both a challenge and an opportunity. After the collapse of the Soviet Union, there was a keen interest in the CARs to reassert their identity. This implied a revival of Islam and nationalism. Often the two were seen as converging, but it soon became apparent that while the people in the CARs wanted Islam as a daily part of their lives, they were by no means eager to foresake their liberal traditions. Thus, they were neither keen to adopt the puritanical life style advocated by the *Wahabis,* or be tied rigidly to the *sharia* as interpreted by the *mullahs.* Thus, religious extremism was supported neither by the people, nor by the ruling elites which considered orthodox Islam as an obstacle in their attempt to modernize, and to retain power. Thus, despite large scale re-building of mosques and *madarsas,* and import of Qurans, the attempt of Iran and Pakistan to export their own version of orthodox Islam had little response, except in Tajikistan where, according to Ahmed Rashid, the jihadi *movement* was more connected with clan rivalries than religious extremism.[10] Turkey, on the other hand, which adhered to secularism and had the advantage of a common language with all the CARs, except Tajikistan adhered to moderate Islam. It also emphasized sufism which had an old tradition and had "kept old religious ritual, prayer and the Muslim inner life distinct and separate from the communist system." They combined Islam with a big programme of training 10,000 students of the region in Turkey's universities, technical colleges and business schools.

However, according to Ahmed Rashid, Turkish influence remained limited because Turkey was seen as "the stalking horse of the Americans." Also, its internal economic collapse and political uncertainties did not provide adequate economic support to the CARs.[11]

It is here that India has an opportunity. India has had a long tradition of having a liberal, humane and pluralistic philosophy of life. It had a strong tradition of sufism, and liberal poets from the time of Amir Khusrau and Faizi to Mirza Ghalib and the present. It had many liberal thinkers and religious leaders who espoused toleration, humanism and egalitarianism. Among moderate Islamic and nationalist thinkers, the name of Maulana Abul Kalam Azad is prominent.

The recent effort of Pervez Musharraf to project Pakistan as a moderate and progressive Islamic state has little credibility either in Pakistan or in the Central Asian Republics. In this context his effort to project himself as an admirer and follower of Kemal Ataturk is significant. While the slogan has few takers in Pakistan, it appears as a transparent effort not only to please the US which has backed

[10]Rashid, Ahmed. 1994. *The Resurgence of Central Asia* Islam or Nationalism? O.U.P. Karachi.

[11]*Ibid. Taliban Islam, Oil and the New Great Game in Central Asia*, I.B. Taurus and Co., London 2001 (revised).

Turkey all along, but also to use the good offices of Turkey to rehabilitate Pakistan in the eyes of the CARs.

Both China and Russia have a deep interest in containing religious extremism in view of the Autonomous Uighur movement in Xinjiang, and the problems Russia faces in Chechnya and other areas in the Russian Federation which have sizeable Muslim populations. With the overthrow of the Taliban regime in Afghanistan, Pakistan remains potentially the most fertile area for breeding Muslim extremism. This, again, is a factor which can provide a basis for closer co-operation and collaboration between Russia, China and India.

Of the neighbouring countries, India and Iran have a close interest in providing an economic outlet to the Central Asian states for the warm water sea-ports for their foreign trade. But, in terms of religion, India has more in common with Turkey than with Iran. Both have an interest in promoting a liberal version of Islam, and have greater credibility of doing so in any of the other neighbouring countries. India is also in a position to provide training in a whole range of fields, from technical education, business management, banking and financial services, not only in an atmosphere more conducive to people from Central Asia, but at a much lower cost than those they would have to incur for training in Western countries.

CHAPTER VIII

Role of Cities in the Growth of an Integrated Hindu-Muslim Culture—A Case Study of Delhi During the Second Half of the 17th and 18th Centuries

The growth of the Muslim civilization in India is intimately associated with the rise of cities. Lahore, Multan, Delhi, Agra, Jaunpur, Nagore, Ajmer, Ahmedabad are only some of the cities which were either established or reached a climax during Muslim rule in India. Many of these cities were not only seats of Government and administration, and of commerce and industry; they also became the centers where a new culture based on a peculiar synthesis of Indian and Muslim values, beliefs and cultural traits, and a broad liberal outlook was fashioned. Jaunpur, for instance, was called the "Shiraz of the East" during the 15th century on account of the large number of savants, writers and artists who had congregated there. Here we are taking up Delhi during the 17th centuries as a case study.

Although Delhi had been an important culture centre during the Sultanat period, it has been relegated to a secondary position with the rise of Agra during the 16th century. Till the middle of the 17th century, both Agra and Lahore outclassed Delhi in size and importance. However, in the eyes of the people, Delhi continued to be looked upon as the real capital (*shahr*), and anyone who aspired to rule India could not ignore it. This, rather than the excessive heat of Agra, and the "march of the Rajasthan desert" accounts for the transfer of the capital from Agra to Delhi by Shah Jahan in 1638.[1]

On account of the keen interest taken by Shah Jahan in promoting artistic activities, and the patronage extended to poets and scholars, both Hindu and Muslim, by Dara Shikoh, Delhi had emerged as an important culture centre by the middle of the 17th century. Aurangzeb, however, evinced little interest in cultural activities. In 1668, he decided to banish music from the court since "his devotion to duty left no time for festivity," but ceremonial music (*naubat*) was continued. He showed little interest in patronage to poets, possibly because he felt that they were too much influenced by sufi mysticism and monism (*wahadat-ul-wajud*). In consequence, he considered them "purveyors of untruth."[2] Aurangzeb also frowned upon painting as un-Islamic. However, this withdrawal of royal patronage to cultural activities resulted only in a limited set back. Literatures and artists who had received encouragement from Mughal Emperors from the time of Akbar downwards, now looked to the inmates of the *haram* and to princes such as Azam and to some of the leading nobles for support and patronage. A number of writers, painters and musicians repaired to provincial centers such as Lahore, Srinagar, Patna, Thatta, Allahabad, etc. and to the courts of autonomous rulers (Amber, Bikaner, Bundi etc.).[3] This implied a wider diffusion of the culture developed

[1]March of the Rajasthan desert, and heat have been suggested by Tavernier (*Travels* p. 86) as the reason for the transfer of capital from Agra to Delhi. (H.K. Naqvi, *Urban Centers*, p. 19, has merely echoed Tavernier's views). As recent scientific studies show, the march of the desert towards Agra is a myth.

[2]*M.A.* 532., The author emphasizes that Aurangzeb was opposed to *qasida-goi* or adulatory verses. But he likes "poems breathing moral advice."

[3]For details, see Nurul Ansari, *Farsi Adab bah Ahd-i-Aurangzeb*, Indo-Persian Society, Delhi, 1969.

at the Mughal court. However, many of the artists were loth to leave Delhi. Chandni Chowk with *Nahr-i-Faiz* flowing down its centre, tall trees lining both sides of the street, and with coffees houses and the dance and music houses which were presided over by well known courtesans well versed in music, poetry and dance, had become a resort for the poets, the artists and the music lovers.[4] After a brief gap, Princess Jahanara, who was highly educated and accomplished, resumed her position at Delhi as the first lady of the realm. She emerged from her self-imposed seclusion after the death of Shah Jahan (1666), and was assigned the house of Ali Mardan Khan— one of the famous houses of Delhi.[5] Aurangzeb fixed a handsome allowance on her. She used her wealth and influence to relieving the distressed, healing discords in the royal family and cultivating the saints, especially the sufi saints. Having been enrolled earlier as a disciple of the liberal sufi saint, Mian Mir of Lahore, she turned her attention to the famous Chishti saint, Shaikh Muinuddin Chishti, and wrote a work, *Munis-ul-Arwah*, on his life. It is almost certain that some of her liberality extended to poets and artists. She continued to live in Delhi and died in 1681.[6] Meanwhile the cultural leadership of Delhi had been assumed by Zeb-un-Nisa, the daughter of emperor Aurangzeb, and by the subahdar of Delhi, Aqil Khan, who

[4]For details, see *Bahar-i-Sukhan*, f.131 a. *Shahjahan Namah*, iii p.29. Aurangzeb banished the dancing girls from Delhi (*M.A.*314)—a step which had been officially taken by earlier rulers also.

Jahandar Shah (1712), it is said, ordered the cutting of lofty trees in Delhi, including those on two banks of the Faiz canal (Khuush-hal 389 b. Irvine, *Later Mughals*, i.194).

[5]Among the other famous houses at Delhi which set a standard, and are referred to by contemporaries were the houses of Mahabat Khan, Ali Mardan Khan, Jafar Khan, Shaista Khan etc. Nurudin Faruqi laments that Jahandar Shah allotted the houses of Mahabat Khan and Ali Mardan Khan to the Kalawants, while Kokaltash Khan occupied the *haveli* of the late wazir, Jafar Khan (*Jahandar Namah* ff.38b-39a).

[6]Jadunath Sarkar, *Aurangzeb's Reign*, Calcutta, 1933, p.144.

bore the pen-name, "Razi." As is well known, Aurangzeb had banished Zeb-un-Nisa to Delhi in 1679 for supporting his rebel son, Prince Akbar. Though a prisoner from 1679 to her death in 1702, she was allowed a good deal of freedom and a sufficient allowance. According to a contemporary, she "appreciated the value of learning and skill; and all her heart were set on the collection, copying and reading of books and she turned her kind attention to improving the lost of scholars as gifted men. The result was that she collected a library, like of which no man has seen; and large number of theologian, scholars, poets, scribes and calligraphists by this means came to enjoy the bounty of this lady hidden in the *harem*." She set up a *bait-ul-ulum* (academy) for the training of artists. Aqil Khan who was a close associate of Aurangzeb was appointed the Governor of Delhi in 1680 and held that post till his death in 1696. An historian and a *masanavi* writer, he had left behind many works of romance: *Mansnavi Mah-o-Mahar* or *Manohar wa Madhumalati, Masanavi Shama-o-Parwana or Padmavati*, etc., *and a Diwan.*[7]

Among the well known poets who had made Delhi their home, and who decided not to leave it in the train of the Mughal court, pride of place may be given to Mirza Abdul Qadir Bedil. Bedil, who was in the service of Prince Azam, resigned his post in 1096 H/1684-85 from Gujarat, and repaired to Delhi, where he spent the next thirty-six years of his life. Bedil was deeply influenced by the mystic poetry of Ibn Arabi and Maulana Rum, and may be considered a liberal, having associated with *sufis* of both types—those who were strictly bound by *shara*, and those who were not. His broad interests were demonstrated by the fact that he knew Hindi well, and knew in full the story of the

[7]*M.A.* 538-39. Niamat Khan Ali, Mulla Saifuddin Qazwini and Mirza Khaliq, were some of the poets and writers associated with her, because their works begin with the word *zeb*, i.e. *Zaib-ul-Tafsir*, *Zaib-ul-Munshaat* etc. (Nurul Ansari, *Ibid*, pp.10-11).

Mahabharata. He was also adept in music. He was closely associated with Aqil Khan "Razi" because of their common interest in *tasawwuf* (mysticism). Bedil, who is considered the leading Persian poet of the age, trained a large number of poets. Soon a school of poets emerged at Delhi. When Bedil died (1720) an annual *urs* began to be organized at his grave where poets would read their new compositions.[8]

The question arises: who patronized the works of these poets? That Delhi was already an important centre of poetry is borne out by the visit to Delhi in 1700 by Wali Deccani (1667-1744). Accompanied by Abul Muali, at Delhi Wali met famous poets and saints, including Sadullah Gulshan, a poet, scholar and saint of Delhi. His poetic works and personality inspired a number of poets at Delhi to use Urdu as a medium of literary expression.[9]

It would appear that during this period a small leisured class of people had emerged at Delhi who had both the means and the taste for giving support and patronage to the cultural activities. Apart from inmates of the *haram*, this included a number of nobles who had settled down at Delhi and made it their home (*watan*). In addition to their pensions, these nobles augmented their incomes by laying out orchards, or building markets (*mandis*). Some of the nobles also participated in trade or let out money on interest, Delhi being one of the biggest money markets in the country. Many businessmen, manufacturers, religious leaders, and *madadd-i-maash* holders had also settled down in Delhi, and gradually acquired a taste for a cultural life. This broadening of the cultural base was a significant factor in the cultural life of Delhi during the 18th century, and the basis on which cultural life at Delhi was continued even when the patronage of the Mughal Emperors was withheld or declined.

[8] Nurul Ansari, *Ibid*, pp. 94-104.
[9] M. Sadiq, *History of Urdu Literature*, p. 62.

It will be seen that during the last quarter of the 17th century, two rival centers, at it were, for the development and transmission of cultural values had emerged—one at Aurangabad, i.e. at the court of Aurangzeb in the Deccan with emphasis on theology, religious studies etc., largely based on the orthodox Hanafi school; and the other at Delhi where the traditions of liberalism initiated by Akbar and Jahangir and which had been nurtured by Dara, were continued and developed further. The role of Delhi as the metropolis of liberalism in the country in the field of culture and religion is significant. During the same period, the tradition of the liberal sufi order, the Chishti *silsilah*, were also sought to be revived at Delhi by Shaikh Kalimullah (1650-1729). He established a *khankah* at Delhi. Attracted by his learning and piety, students from different parts of the country flocked to him. The Shaikh was simultaneously initiated into a number of *silsilahs*—the Chishti or the Suharawardiya, and the Qadiriya. He advocated monotheism (*wahdat-ul-wujud*) and *sama* (music) in mystic gatherings, using Hindi songs. He made it his life's mission to counter the orthodox Naqshbandiya order. His student, Shaikh Nizam-ud-Din who had settled at Aurangabad, and his son Shah Fakhr-ud-Din returned to Delhi and settled there to continue his mission.[10]

As has been mentioned above, Jahanara had devoted herself to the growth and revival of the Chishti order at Delhi towards the end of her life. Visiting the tombs of saints, especially on special occasions such as their *urs* became one of the favourite past times of the Delhi populace. The orthodox elements, as is well known, frowned upon these practices, but their continuance and growing popularity showed the wide diffusion of *sufi* ideas and beliefs. These in turn, coincided with many Hindu ideas and

[10]S.A.A. Rizvi, *Shah Wali Allah and his Times,* Marifat Publishing House, Australia, 1980, pp. 360-62, 369-77.

practices so that both Muslims and Hindus visited the tombs of *sufi* saints and participated in their *urs*.

Delhi passed through a number of phases during the 18th century. The Mughal emperor, Bahadur Shah (1707-12), the son and successor of Aurangzeb who had never entered Delhi, came to live at Delhi. Thus, Delhi welcomed the Mughal Emperor after a gap of 33 years, following the departure of Aurangzeb to Ajmer and then to the Deccan in 1679. Between 1712 and the invasion of Nadir Shah in 1739, civil wars and faction fights, recurrent famine and pestilence, and growing administrative laxity which further accentuated the financial problems facing the Government and the ruling classes and a growing threat from the Marathas could not, however, seriously deter Delhi from forging ahead in the field of cultural development, and further strengthening and broadening its liberal traditions. Though the political extent of the Mughal Empire diminished and so did the revenue resources which could be used by the Emperor and the nobility, the reign of Muhammad Shah (1720-48) was outwardly a period of cultural brilliance. During the period, Delhi, emerged as the unrivalled centre of Indo-Mughal culture. Architecture took a back-seat and painting remained largely repetitive, but the real glory of this period lies in the field of literature and music, and in the consolidation of the traditions of an urbane, humanistic, broad-based culture, largely free from sectarianism or narrow religious bias. While Persian continued to be patronized by a section of the upper classes, Urdu began to emerge as a language of the classes and the masses. Thus, among the Urdu poets of the period mention may be made of Muhammad Aman Nisar, a musician; Husain Bakhshi, a cloth merchant; Madan Singh Shaguftah, a goldsmith; Shambu Nath Aziz, a banker, and Mir Sadiq Ali Sadiq who was a broker.[11]

[11]M. Sadiq, *ibid*.

Emperor Muhammad Shah, and some of his leading nobles, such as the wazir, Qamar-ud-Din Khan; the Mir Bakhshi Khan-i-Dauran, etc. must be given the credit of secludously fostering and patronizing this liberal and humanistic tradition in which both Muslims and Hindus participated. The spirit of Muhammad Shah may be illustrated by an example. At Delhi, a Hindu had embraced Islam. After some time, he decided to revert to Hinduism, whereupon an agitated crowd of Muslims demonstrated against it at the Friday prayers, and demanded his death, since punishment for apostasy was death. The matter was brought to the Emperor, Muhammad Shah, who referred it to the Shaikh-ul-Islam. The Shaikh-ul-Islam dismissed the plaint on the ground that it was a personal matter. Muhammad Shah accepted the advise of the Shaikh-ul-Islam, but to quell the agitation, he had the Hindu spirited out of Delhi and to appease the orthodox elements, removed the Shaikh-ul-Islam from his post.[12]

The pillage, plunder and massacre perpetrated by Nadir Shah at Delhi in 1739 was a profound shock to rich and poor alike. Even more disturbing were the recurrent Abdali invasions from 1756 onwards and the cruelties perpetrated on the royal family by Ghulam Qadir. But with the return of Shah Alam II to Delhi in 1774 under the protection of Mahadji Sindhia, Delhi rapidly recovered its position as a centre for commerce and culture.

Writing in 1194 H/1780, the author of the *Maasir-ul-Umara* says:

"Nadir Shah's occupation resulted in a set back to the prosperity of the city, but in a short while it returned to normal, and in fact in everything it is now better and shows progress. A description of its decoration is not possible for the pen: its industries and manufactures are flourishing, and

[12]Rustam Ali *Tarikh-i-Hindi*: Elliot and Dowson, VIII, p.52.

music and convivial meetings are a common feature of the life of people."[13]

Thus, the attempt of British historians and following that of some modern historians to paint the entire 18th century as a period of great anarchy and economic decline, and to dub the entire 18th century as a period of "unchecked decline" for Delhi is not warranted by facts.

To some extent, the picture of the depopulation and ruination of Delhi, the decline of trade and manufacture, the penury of the nobles and their dependents including the soldiers and the professions, and the flight of poets and artists to other climes in search of patronage is based on the writings of Urdu poets, such as Sauda, especially on their *Shahr Ashobs*. As is known, the tradition of writing *Shahr-Ashob* was an old one.[14]

Writing on the condition of Delhi during the brief period of civil war following the illness of Shah Jahan, Bahishti tells us how all the crafts and professions had been ruined, and social values were collapsing. Jafar Zatalli, writing during the latter part of Aurangzeb's reign, not only dwells on the difficulty of getting employment, but rues that the norms of society were breaking down, those in service could not make the two ends meet, soldiers were heavily in debt to *mahajans* and were selling their weapons, people of mean professions the cotton carder, the weaver, the vegetable seller and the butcher, etc. were well off, and people of low castes (*rajal*) were getting preference.[15] The same theme is to be found in the *Shahr Ashobs* written in the 18th century. Thus, due allowance should be made for poetic exaggeration. The citizens of Delhi showed a remarkable capacity for facing adversity, and

[13]*Maasir-ul-Umara*, tr. Baini Prasad, Vol. II, p. 273.

[14]Naim Ahmad, *Shahr Ashab ka Tahqiqi Matala*, Aligarh, 1959, pp.17-25, loc.cit. *Essays* pp. 82-83.

[15]Naim Ahmad, *Kulliyat-i-Jafar Zatalle*, Aligarh, 1977.

begueathed a literary and cultural tradition which continued apace till the middle of the 19th century and even later.

Within the framework of a feudal society, the culture that was developed in Delhi during the first half of the 18th century was as broad-based as possible. Urdu poetry absorbed not only some of the best traditions of Persian, many Urdu poets also composing in Hindi.

Thus, Urdu verse emerged as the best representative of an integrated culture. In their writings, the word "brahaman" signified a true devotee as opposed to a "shaikh" who was considered a hypocrite, and the temple (*but-khana*) the abode of true faith. Emphasis on the outer forms of religious belief which was insisted upon by the *mullahs* was also held up to ridicule. Thus, Nasikh says:

Kufr Islam ko kuch paid nahin ae Atish
Shaikh ho ya ki brahaman ho wah insan hoe.

(*Kufr* and Islam have little aversion to each other, since both shaikh and brahmans are human beings.)

Despite efforts to reverse this tradition by a few narrow theologians, such was the humane and secular tradition fostered by Delhi, and by many other cities of the time.

CHAPTER IX

Integration, Dynamism and Stagnation in Indian Culture and Raja Ram Mohan Roy

I have deliberately chosen the title in order to place Ram Mohan Roy in the Indian tradition of periodic re-interpretations of a highly structural society based on a divinely ordained moral law, as well as to the social developments of the time. In the Indian theory of *yugas*, or ages, change is central. It is not only the moral law that changes, all aspects of society and its institutions are susceptible to the law of change. This at once set up a contradiction between the Vedas which were supposed to be eternal and immutable, and the processes of change which were also continuous, and could not be denied. Little effort was made to resolve this contradiction, so that the pendulum swung from one end to the other, according to concrete conditions. Hence, periods of change and periods of stagnation in the cultural field.

Raja Ram Mohan Roy has been variously hailed as the first "Indian Patriot," as the initiator of social reform in Hindu Society, and as a great humanist who tried to bring together all religions, especially Hinduism, Islam and Christianity. He has also been described as "the first plant which grew as a result of the dissemination of western culture in the Indian Soil." (Tara Chand).

It is unfortunate that in most of our text-books, Ram Ram Mohan Roy is shown as a reformer who was largely influenced both positively and negatively, by Christianity and Christian missionaries and, to some extent, by Macaulay and Macaulayism. This is to some extent, a continuation of the belief propagated by men like James Mill that the entire Indian civilization and culture was utterly debased, and incapable of any rational urgings. Hence all elements of development and rationality had to be looked for outside India. It was on this account that during the 19th century, men like Weber, Caldwell, Pope, Grierson, Fawcett, etc. tried to trace the origins of the Bhakti Movement in South India between the 7th and the 11th centuries to Christianity, and Barth, Senart etc, to Islam. Later, Percy Brown traced all developmental aspects in Medieval Indian architecture to Iran or Central Asia or the West, though he did not repeat the belief held by an earlier generation of British historians and travellers that Taj Mahal was built by an Italian architect.

In a symposium held at Delhi in 1973 to mark the second birth centenary of Raja Ram Mohan Roy, an attempt was made by a number of contributors to trace the intellectual development of Ram Mohan Roy, and to bring out the Indian background to Ram Mohan's intellectual development. Dr. A.K. Majumdar emphasized, and the editor, Prof. Rajat Ray, noted the "three main influences in Rammohan's thought—Persian, Vedantic and Occidental—(which) were imbibed by him successively strictly in that chronological order."

The precise extent of the impact of Islam and Perso-Arabic learning on the one hand, and Vedant on the other on Raja Ram Mohan Roy's thinking is still a matter of speculation since little work has been done so far to bring out the nature of the social, cultural and intellectual intercourse between the Hindu and Muslim upper classes —the *shurfa* and the *bhadralok*, during the 18th century. As is well known, monotheism and idol worship were two important issues which divided the Hindus and Muslims right from the incursion of Islam into India. Al-Biruni, the most noted

Arabic scholar of Hinduism, had pointed out towards the end of the 9th and beginning of the 10th century, that the educated Hindus "consider the unity of God as absolute, but that everything besides God which may appear as a unity is really a plurality of things," ... and that "(they) are entirely free from worshipping an image manufactured to represent him." However, Al-Biruni's words did not have much impact on the attitude of the Turkish ruling classes and theologians towards the Hindus and Hinduism. It was profitable for the Turkish invaders to plunder the richly endowed Hindu temples in the name of destroying idolatory, and to gain religious merit for doing so, because in practice, the mass of the Hindus were sunk in gross superstition, with many of them wedded to all kinds of esoteric and immoral practices and beliefs which had received religious sanction. A religion of works emphasizing worship of God in different forms, was of direct benefit to the Brahmans—as Ram Mohan Roy was to point out in a famous tract more than 800 years later. Kabir and Nanak who wanted to bring the two main communities, the Hindus and the Muslims, together, instinctively realized the importance of laying emphasis on the concept of an attributeless supreme spirit and opposing image-worship, and with it, the theory of incarnation of God in human form. As Ram Mohan Roy noted, "..... followers of Cabeer and Nanak do worship God without the assistance of consecrated objects." However, after shocking the orthodox and creating a stir, the followers of Kabir had shrunk into a sect. The influence of Nanak proved to be more lasting, but Sikhism became a force only during the 18th century. Even then the influence of the Sikhs remained confined largely to the Punjab. Saguna Bhakti, the mystical movement based on the adoration of Shiva or Vishnu in the forms of Rama or Krishna, swept the rest of the country, and remained dominant during the 17th and 18th centuries.

This is not the place to attempt to examine in detail the positive and negative aspects of this aspect of the bhakti movement, and its Islamic counterpart, the sufi movement. While both tried to free religion from external trammels or of a stultifying credo, and laid emphasis on the psycho-emotional and ethical aspects of religion, they created new superstitions in the form of guru worship (or worship of the grave of the *pirs*), and pushed the rational-intellectual processes to the background. Love for God in whatever form did provide a platform for the Hindus and the Muslims to come together, and, to that extent, overcoming some of their prejudices towards each other. This provided a basis for political integration, but the anti-intellectual basis was a barrier to a deeper study and understanding of the two communities on a firm, rational basis. The anti-intellectualism had, as well, implications in other branches of life. Thus, during the 16th, 17th and 18th centuries, the Muslim and Hindu upper classes which were deeply influenced by Sufism and the Vaishnavism neglected this study of science and technology and other rational sciences. Akbar's attempt to reform the traditional syllabus by introducing secular subjects such as mathematics was not successful, and the syllabus of the Dars-i-Nizamiyah emphasizing theology, jurisprudence, *fiqh*, etc. remained the norm. It was this syallbus that Ram Mohan Roy must have studied at Patna where he had been sent for learning Persian. The Mughal Emperors borrowed priests and brass guns from the Protuguese and the English, but did not learn from them the principles of mechanics and physics which were beginning to transform western society. Tipu did set up ordnance factories and manufactories in Mysore during the 18th century, but lacking knowledge of modern science and technology in the country, they were bound to fail, and did fail.

The lack of proper intellectual/rational atmosphere in the country may explain not only the failure of a rational king like Muhammad bin Tughlaq, but also the fact that between the 10th and 18th centuries, only three or four serious efforts were made to understand Islam and Hinduism, viz, that by Al-Biruni, that by Abul Fazl aided by Akbar, and that by Dara followed, to some extent, by Mirza Mazhar *Jan-i-Janan* during the 18th century. From the side of the Hindus, Ram Mohan Roy was, perhaps, the first who attempted this task in his Persian work, *Tuhfat-ul-Mujahidin*. His Persian writings, therefore, need ever greater attention and careful study than has been given to them so far.

Over-emphasis on the political processes and the neglect of social and cultural processes had led to a tacit acceptance of the essence of the two nation theory, viz, that during the pre-British period or even up to recent times, the Hindus and the Muslims who inhabited the same territories lived as two distinct entities, with a minimum of social and cultural interchange between them. As usual, the western scholars have buttressed this argument with reference to the caste system. It has been argued that caste taboos did not permit the Hindus and the Muslims to inter-marry or to inter-dine, and that this was the most potent factor which kept the Muslims a separate element in India over the centuries. A brief comparison with Europe would show the fallacy of this argument. In France and Germany, Catholics and Protestants have maintained their separate identities, though caste does not emerge as a barrier there. The experience of the Jews—as also of Shiites in many lands, show that where a religious or ethnic minority is determined to maintain its separate identity, it can contrive to do so. Thus caste *alone* cannot be considered the determining factor in social relations. A whole range of motives, attitudes and values must be studied *along* with caste to determine the actual relations between the two communities. And this has to be done in relation to time and space since motives, attitudes and values can and do differ and change over time.

Regarding values and attitudes of the Muslims and Hindus, Aurangzeb's reign must be considered a water-shed in a sense different from what has been the general understanding: rather than being considered a period in which a number of steps were taken to reverse Akbar's policy of cultural integration, it should rather be seen as a phase which marked the last attempt of the orthodox ulema to use state power to assert their hold over the Muslim community, and to use the *sharia* as a means to establish a state based on the privileges of a narrow group depending on birth and prescriptive rights. This attempt suffered from a number of serious limitations from the beginning. On political grounds, Aurangzeb declined to oust the Hindus from the nobility, as well from subordinate services. As the economic and political crisis deepened, he tried to open avenues to government service for the Muslim lower middle classes by restricting employment to the Hindus. At the same time, he had to induct large number of Marathas in to the nobility, raising the proportion of the Hindus to almost a third—far higher than it ever had been before. This added to the problem of employment for the sons and sons-in-law of the old "Turani" and "Irani" nobles, the *khanazads*. Even his earlier policy of not permitting new temples and enforcing *jizyah* had to be modified by Aurangzeb in the latter part of his reign. Thus *jizyah* was suspended in 1704 in the entire Deccan on the ground of the "distressed condition of the cultivators" due to famine and the war with the Marathas. It could never be revived. Five years after Aurangzeb's death, in 1712, *jizyah* was formally abolished by Jahandar Shah at the instance of Asad Khan—the wazir, and a favourite of Aurangzeb. A subsequent effort of Nizam-ul-Mulk Asaf Jah, the founder of Hyderabad state, to revive *jizyah* also failed.

As Mughal power declined during the 18th century, a number of significant developments took place. First, the Mughal Emperor gradually ceased to be the patron of orthodoxy, but of liberal arts and cultural integration. The change was begun hesitantly by Bahadur Shah, and carried forward by Jahandar Shah and Farrukh Siyar. It was brought to a head by Muhammad-Shah, who reigned for 28 long years. Generally remembered as a weak man devoted to a life of sensuality, he should be given credit for encouraging new forms of music to which both Muslims and Hindus contributed, to literature—both Persian and Urdu, and to painting. He was also a great patron of the liberal Sufis, and angered and annoyed the orthodox elements by permitting a Hindu who had embraced Islam to revert to his old faith. The orthodox elements had demanded death to the apostate, and created a public stir. It is interesting that the Shaikh-ul-Islam held that religion was a personal affair—which, as we know, is the basic principle of secularism. Muhammad Shah's support to cultural integration coincided with a virtual collapse of the empire, and with it of the composite ruling class which had emerged under the fostering care of the Mughals and which is one of their significant contribution. A composite ruling class analogous to it could not be created in any of the successor principalities such as Hyderabad, Awadh or Bengal, though individual Hindus continued to enjoy position of trust and power, at various levels, especially administration and for collection of land revenue.

Similarly, while individual Muslim nobles or commanders found favour with some of the Maratha chiefs and Rajput rulers, no attempt was made to develop a composite ruling class. But this did not lead to a set back to the processes of cultural integration. Mughal "high" culture had already been assimilated to some extent, by the Rajput ruling elements. In order to gain social respectability, it was avidly copied by the Maratha ruling elements also. Upper class Hindus in Hyderabad, Awadh, and Bengal did not find any cultural barriers in co-mingling with the Muslim ruling elite.

This was paralleled by a subtler, even more important development. This was the emergence of a new class of landholders and middle man,—zamindars, talluqedars, *ijaredars* etc., drawn from miscellaneous social groups such as the smaller nobles, military adventures, village chaudharis, petty revenue officials (qanungo, *sarrishidars*), *madadd-i-maash* (rent free land) holders, traders, etc. consisting of both Hindus and Muslims. It was this social formation—I hesitate to call it a class because of its disparate origins and internal differences—which gradually emerged as an important element, and, to a considerable extent, set the cultural tone in these newly emerged principalities. The family of Raja Ram Mohan Roy also belonged to this new social grouping, his father having worked as a *sarishtedar* for the Begum at Murshidabad. It should thus be seen that the eclipse of many of the old landed families, and the rise of new landed elements in Bengal since 1765, leading to considerable vicissitudes in the fortunes of individual families, was not something which developed simply as a result of British policies and attitudes. The process had started earlier. British policies accentuated the trend, capped by the *Permanent Settlement.*

The values and attitudes of this new social group which may broadly be called the lower gentry had its moorings in the countryside, but its face was towards the city. In Kotah, Bundi, as also in Eastern Rajasthan we have instances of urban traders being granted *ijara istimarar*, i.e, lands on contract for a long period. Significantly, the word *istimarar* did *not*, under the Mughals, imply a permanent right. In fact, it would not be far wrong to assert that under the Mughals no rights were permanent; not only had the succession of an autonomous ruler to the *gaddi* to be approved by the ruler, all *madadd-i-maash* and similar grants which were granted from "generation to generation" had to be renewed by each successor, as well by each succeeding sovereign. But to come back to the point, in Bengal where there was a strong trading tradition, the displacement of old zamindari families and the induction of traders and lower administrators as zamindars or contractors was a continuous process. The induction of lower revenue officials, *madadd-i-maash* holders, etc., in this hereditary class has been studied in the context of Awadh, Eastern Rajasthan and also in Bengal, but in a somewhat haphazard manner, without drawing necessary conclusions.

The rural lower gentry had its counterpart in the city. Towards the end of the 17th century, there emerged in cities such as Delhi and Agra a leisured class which had resigned or disdained the service of the emperor, living on the income of orchards, rent from markets (*mandis*), loans to merchants etc. This class had sufficient means to extend patronage to the Urdu poets, musicians, etc. who were denied support by Aurangzeb and the orthodox elements. This circle gradually grew, specially when Urdu became a literary language and could appeal to a broader section. The role of Urdu in the process of acculturation, of introducing larger sections across the country to Mughal culture which was based on Muslim and Hindu values and concepts has not been adequately appreciated by historians. Apart from Delhi, Agra, Lucknow, etc. centers of Urdu poetry developed during the 18th century at provincial centers such as Srinagar, Lahore, Allahabad, Hyderabad, Patna, etc. Many of the early poets of Urdu were broad-minded humanists. They drew on Hindu traditions, a few of them composing in Hindi also. Almost all of them took a stand against Muslim orthodoxy, equating the "brahman" to the believer and *kufr* to the true faith. Thus, Sauda roundly declared that true faith was in no way opposed to infidelity. He says:

"*Ghar kufr se khuhh nah hai din se matlab*
(*Kufr* or infidelity have nothing to do with *din* or faith)

Atish went so far as to say:
"But khanah tor daliye
Masjid ko dhaiye
Dil ko nah toriye
Yeh khudah ka maqam hai."
(Break the temples, and uproot the mosques, But do not break anyone's heart for that is the abode of God).

Let me draw together what I have been trying to say. My point is that Muslim orthodoxy could never make any considerable headway among the Muslim ruling classes. The narrow views of Shaikh Ahmad Sirhindi made little impact, and the orthodoxy-favouring policies of Aurangzeb came a cropper in his own life time. Under Muhammad Shah, the Mughal ruler re-emerged as the leader of cultural integration. But the empire could not be saved and the Mughal composite ruling class which had been the standard bearer of cultural integration collapsed. Its place was, however, taken by a new social group which, for purposes of convenience, may be called the lower gentry. This class had been deeply influenced by Mughal culture, so much so that Persian was almost a *lingua franca* among them. Thus, many of them, such as Chander Bhan Barhman, Ishwardas Nagar, Bhimsen, Lachhmi Narayan Shafiq, to name a few, emerged as writers of Persian history and literature. Although Sanskrit and Hindi (or Bengali or the local literary language) was cultivated by many of them, quite a few of them—specially in modern Punjab, U.P., Bihar, preferred to read even their scriptures such as the Ramayana and the Mahabharata in the Persian script. Extant survivals in libraries and personal collections would bear this out.

The religious and cultural values of this group were very miscellaneous. While deeply religious, and committed to their traditional faiths and their value system, they also drew on Mughal traditions of humanism and urbanism.

Side by side with respecting saints and *pirs*, they were influenced by the Vedantik tradition of monotheism, or the Persian tradition of *wahadat-al-wajud*. Implicitly rather than explicitly this implied denial of the worship of God through symbolic objects, i.e, idols. But such a radical conclusion was rarely drawn, eclecticism being the norm. In general, these sections were keen to raise their social status through a process of "Sanskritization." This may explain why the practice of "Sati" grew during thc 18th century.

All these contradictory aspects are to be found in the early life and intellectual development of Raja Ram Mohan Roy. Given his traditional training in Persian and Sanskrit, and employed as a revenue official till 1815, there was nothing in Ram Mohan's thinking till he reached Calcutta to show that he was far different from others drawn from his background and his class. His defence of the rights of women—their right to property, opposition to multiple marriages by Kulin brahmans, child marriages, the education and degradation of widows and of course, opposition to *Sati*, belong, however, to both the early and the later phase. We have yet to trace more clearly the sources of his inspiration in this field which had the most far reaching repercussions and which set him out as a social reformer. Support of women's rights appears most clearly in his *Second Defence of the Monotheistic System of the Vedas* written in 1817 where he condemned the "modern brahmans" to be full of guile to force women to commit *sati*, child marriages, multiple marriages by brahmans (*kulinism*), etc. Neither Islam in India, nor Vedantism nor medieval mysticism had much to contribute in this field. It can be traced partially to the humane influence of John Digby, and partly to logic which Ram Mohan Roy learnt from the Naiyyaiks which had been traditionally strong in Bengal. But this needs a more careful study.

It is curious that while Ram Mohan Roy's advocacy of social reform has been rightly highlighted, his equally trenchant criticism of British rule in India, and his strong denunciation of British agrarian policies has not received as much attention. In his Preface to the first *Brahmanical Magazine*, Ram Mohan noted that in Bengal "the mere name of Englishman is sufficient to frighten people." In the course of his *Exposition of Judicial and Revenue System* in 1831, he observed that the British stood "isolated in the midst of its subjects, supporting itself merely by the exertion of superior force." For those who have recently been arguing that British rule in India stood on the "consent of the people," these remarks by one considered to be a friend by the British are interesting.

Regarding the economic impact of British rule, Ram Mohan Roy noted that it was "a system which at once presses down the people and exhausts the resources of the country." Likewise, he condemned both the zamindari, i.e, the Permanent Settlement and the Ryotwari System, saying: "Under both systems, the condition of the cultivator is very miserable; in the one, they are placed at the mercy of the zamindars' avarice and ambition; in the other they are subjected to the extortions and intrigues of the surveyors and other government revenue officers." Hence, his radical demand for the reductions of rents.

I would not like to expand on this, or to try to touch here on the influence of the Benthamite Radical Humanism on Ram Mohan Roy. The analysis of the 18th century social background, leads me to believe that Ram Mohan Roy can hardly be called a representative of a nascent Indian or Bengali bourgeoisie. Rather, he can better be called the representative of the lower gentry that was trying to displace the older gentry, and had received and expected the support of the British bourgeoisie in this task. The fact of some of the members of this class becoming brokers, *dallals* of the British did not really change their basic character. That may explain why the so-called Bengal Renaissance could not strike roots or spread out from Bengal. The class in Bengal on which it was based was only interested in emerging as a full-fledged landed class, displacing the old landed class. It could do so once agricultural prices, and with it, the value of land, reached a level at which those who had bought land under the rules of the Permanent Settlement could meet without any undue difficulty the high level at which Cornwallis had fixed the land-revenue demand. A genuine awakening had thus to await the turn of the century when a native bourgeoisie had reached a certain stage of development. It was then that Ram Mohan Roy was virtually re-discovered, and his call for social reform and women's emancipation incorporated in the national programme. Nevertheless, his more radical message of rationalism, of land-reform and of providing relief to the cultivator, and of emphasis on modern science had to await the growth of greater mass awakening and of the rise of socialist ideas in the country with which the name of Jawaharlal Nehru is closely linked.

From the foregoing review, it would be apparent that period of economic and intellectual-cultural growth do not always coincide. When they do—as happened in the Gupta Age, or during the Age of Akbar, we have what people like to call a "golden age," but one that an historian would like to call an age of growth and awakening. When they pull in opposite or disparate directions—as happened in the 11th and the 19th centuries, there is a measure of economic growth on one hand but little awakening, in the other, an awakening but little economic growth. We find these peculiar anomalies, and hence contradictions in Raja Ram Mohan Roy, *and* in our study of Raja Ram Mohan Roy.

All in all, it would appear that Raja Ram Mohan Roy was both contemporary and one who was born far in advance of his times. He fights once again the old battle between monotheism and polytheism, of iconoclasm and idol-worship, of religious narrowness and a broad humanism. He also pin-points the issues on which a national consciousness was to emerge later on—representative government, administrative reforms, relief to cultivator, etc. On the occasion of the 216th Birth Anniversary of the Raja, I would like to pay my humble tribute to him—a great humanist, a rationalist, a synthesizer of traditions, and a seminar figure who sowed seeds which were to germinate and flower long after his death.

CHAPTER X

The Uprising of 1857—Its Nature and Consequences*

The Centenary of the Uprising of 1857—dubbed the Sepoy Mutiny by English historians—has seen a number of publications which have attempted to analyse the nature and underlying causes of the event. A good deal of fresh material has been unearthed, and light thrown on a number of obscure and controversial points. Nevertheless, many important problems yet remain to be discussed. Little attempt has so far been made to pose the "Mutiny" against the background of the changing socio-economic pattern, to study the attitude and the role of the various classes in it, and to assess its impact on the Indian mind and society during the succeeding years.

Even a cursory analysis of the causes of the "Mutiny" makes it obvious that it was the inevitable result of a hundred years of British rule since the Battle of Plassey. To a modern Indian observer, what appears surprising is not that the "Mutiny" should have occurred, but that it should have been so late in coming.

THE CAUSES

The causes of the unpopularity of English rule had been observed and commented upon by an Indian historian, Ghulam Husain, as early as 1783. After criticizing the character of the English officials, their habit of mixing up

*Written in 1957 to mark the Centenary of the Uprising.

private and public affairs, their ignorance of Indian languages and customs, the slow and costly nature of their legal proceedings, their support and encouragement of zamindars "who are to a man, a refractory short sighted, faithless set of people," the neglect of arts and crafts, the distress caused by the disbanding of Indian armies, etc., the author remarks that the conquerors of India are divided into two categories, "those who did not intend to stay, and thought only of slaughter or plunder, made haste to display the standard of return, and to be gone, as soon as they had got plunder and booty enough to gratify their avarice. But there were others ... intending to settle forever ... lent the whole strength of their genius in securing the happiness of the new subjects; nor did they abate anything to their efforts, until they had intermarried with the natives, and got children and families from them, and become naturalized. Their immediate successors having learnt the language of the country, behaved to its inhabitants as brothers of one mother and one language...."

THE CRUX OF THE PROBLEM

The author has here put his finger on the crux of the problem. The English, though foreigners like many other conquerors who had invaded India previous to them, refused to be absorbed by the country. They stood aloof from the local people, and their interest was centred not in the country but outside it. Hence the fundamental contradiction between their interests and the interests of the people. This contradiction grew progressively sharper, and could be solved only at the expense of the Indian people, or with the expulsion of the English from the country.

We need not go here into the early agrarian experiments of the English. They attempted to reproduce the counterpart of the Whig aristocracy in Bengal, and completely ignored the old aristocracy, the *bhadralok* in Bengal and the Polygars in Madras. Their determination to extract the full "economic" rent led everywhere to over-assessment, the ruination of the old aristocracy, and the reduction of the peasant to the most abject levels. The cash nexus, and the bourgeois concept of property revolutioned the old relations. The *bania* became the dominant element in village society, and large areas of land passed into the hands of money-lenders, commission agents, vakils, and the like.

"DEVIL'S" ENGINE

The steady development of the Industrial Revolution in England, the unfavourable excise policy, and the distress of the upper classes spelled the ruination of the flourishing urban handicrafts. The abolition of the East India Company's trade monopoly in 1833, and the subsequent introduction of the railway system under Dalhousie, opened the interior of the country to the penetration of Lancashire textiles. It was not altogether without reason that the peasant called the railway "the devil's engine," and saw in it an instrument for riveting more firmly the bond of a hated alien rule.

Nor were the upper classes contented. Arthur Wellesley, the brother of Lord Wellesley, had stated long ago that British conquest implied that the former ruling class was "excluded from all share of emolument, honour and authority." Under the East India Company, no Indian could rise above the rank of subahdar in the army and a deputy collector in civil employ. High prices, always considered as "a peculiar curse of British raj," increased the misery of the upper classes and the urban population.

RELATIONSHIP CHANGES

The changed economic and political relationship between India and Britain did not remain unnoticed by British officials. Bentink sadly observed that racial superiority had grown to such an extent that "on going to a station, no Englishman thought of calling on the notables of the district, as was once done as a matter of course; instead certificates of respectability were required of notables before they could be guaranteed a chair when they visited the officer." Men of Macaulay's generation were impatient of those who advocated the preservation of Indian culture, and sincerely believed that the greatest benefit England could confer upon India was to help in producing a generation of people "Indian in colour and blood but English in taste, in opinions, in morals and in intellect." Hence religion and politics became twin weapons for the attainment of a common objective. District officials saw nothing wrong in encouraging missionaries. The reaction against conversions and missionaries—though grossly exaggerated—was simultaneously a reaction against the insidious efforts to undermine and destroy Indian culture.

A forward policy in the political sphere led to the annexation of Sindh and the Punjab, the Afghan War, and the notorious doctrine of Lapse. In 1841, the Court of Directors adopted the famous Minute that the right to political succession was an indulgence which should be the exception and not the rule, and that the Company should "persevere in the one clear and direct course of abandoning no just and honourable accession of territory or revenue...." This doctrine, as implemented by Dalhousie, thoroughly alarmed the princes. The landed elements were already chafing at the working of the Inam commission which had deprived them of large areas of land—a good portion of it ill-gotten.

NATURE OF THE "MUTINY"

Thus, the middle of the century saw unrest pervade all spheres of Indian life and society. The story of the greased cartridges, therefore, acted as spark to the powder keg. It brought together into one movement elements and classes which had no common bond except the expulsion of the British. This was the source of both strength and weakness of the uprising.

English historians have made much of the part played by the sepoys in the Mutiny to cover up the people's verdict against British rule. No such popular uprising as the Mutiny had ever taken place against the Mughals, nor even against the Turkish Sultans. Thus the uprising was a condemnation of British rule as compared to both of them.

It is undoubtedly true that without the revolt of the sepoys a popular uprising of such a magnitude could hardly have taken place. The reason for this was not contentment under British rule, but a complete absence of an independent political leadership. Dr. S.N. Sen and Dr. Mazumdar have convincingly shown that Nana, the Rani of Jhansi, Bahadur Shah and others neither planned nor were capable of planning a movement like the Mutiny which, in this sense, was "unpremedited." Individuals like Maulvi Ahmadulla Shah openly proclaimed their desire to root out British rule, but they were never considered a serious threat to the British Government, and were allowed to function with remarkable freedom. But once the sepoys had risen, the fires of popular discontentment against the British kept the rebellion going. In many places peasant uprisings in the districts preceded the rebellion of the garrisons of sepoys. It is not surprising that an ill-planned, uncoordinated, spontaneous outburst like the Mutiny failed. What is remarkable is that a movement of this nature should have brought a highly organized and economically superior government so near the verge of defeat.

POPULAR

Thus, the Mutiny was essentially a popular uprising sparked by a rebellion in the ranks of the Company's Indian troops which had become the mainstay of the British government, and developing into almost a national effort to throw off the shackles of foreign domination. But that does not mean it had no inner contradictions. These prevented the uprising from developing a full-fledged national character and also ensured its failure.

The first contradiction was between the nation-wide character of the discontent and the absence of the necessary means and organization for giving the discontent a nation-wide expression. The idea of an Indian nation was, as yet, only in its embryonic stage. There was no class or element capable of binding together the peasant discontent into a common organization. Hence, peasant discontent took the form of sporadic uprising, such as the Santhal uprising of 1855-56, Indigo Planters' uprising of 1860, and later the Deccan and the Moplah uprising, etc. The Mutiny was one more such uprising, this time of the peasants in North West India. But the peasants had no idea about the true character and strength of the British Government. Thus, it was fondly believed that the bulk of Englishmen had already migrated to India, and that the English could consequently, get no reinforcements from Home. Hence, they busied themselves in dealing with their local oppressors, and in recovering the land which the village *bania* and other unscrupulous elements had filched from them.[1]

THE SECOND CONTRADICTION

The second contradiction was between the sepoy and the rest of the civil population. The sepoy army was a mercenary army, with a great pride in its profession, and zealously

[1]c/f the remark of Raikes, *Notes on the Revolt in the N.W. Provinces of India* (London 1858):

"Native bankers and merchants, who had long been investing their savings in land (purchased generally under decrees of courts), were either murdered or scared away. The life of a capitalist or mortgagee, was soon not worth a week's purchase."

attached to its privileges. While the prevailing peasant discontent—especially in East U.P. from where the bulk of the Bengal Army was recruited—effected them in some degree, the prime cause of their disaffection was the British attempt to curtail their privileges, and to recruit a fresh army from the Punjabis and Gurkhas. The changed attitude of the British also made them less inclined to put up with the caste prejudices of the Sepoys. The rebellious sepoy could not discard a life-time's habit of looking upon the civil population as a rabble which could be imposed upon and ordered about. He failed, except in some cases, to realize the need for a new, revolutionary discipline, while breaking away from that of the foreign masters. The certitude of merciless reprisal from the British in case of defeat also made him harsh and ruthless at times. Atrocities begot counter-atrocities—though it is difficult to say who started them first, the sepoys or the British officers. But unnecessary harshness discredited the "mutineers," and neutralized a section of the middle-class which might have otherwise thrown in its lot with the popular forces.

ALIGNMENT OF CLASSES

By far the most important contradiction, however, was that between the popular movement and its leadership. In the absence of an independent peasant leadership, there were basically only two classes capable of assuming the leadership of the movement: the middle class, or the landed aristocracy.

The middle class can be divided into two broad sections. One of them consisted of the descendents of the oligarchy and professional classes of the Mughal period who had in many cases found employment in the Indian States. This section lived in the past, dreamt of a return of the old days, and spent its time in cultivating poetry or in religious researches. Some elements of this section, such as Maulvi

Ahmadulla Shah of Fyzabad and others who were formerly in the service of the Nawabs of Awadh, threw in their lot with the "mutineers," and were often the best organizers.

The other and also the bigger section of the middle class, however, was the one which served the British in various subordinate capacities and acted as their trade and commission agents and out of which a small professional class was gradually rising. This class had benefited most from the British agrarian policy and legal set-up, and acquired a considerable amount of agricultural property in many areas, such as Bengal. It was thus not a full-fledged middle class, having feudal interests and ambitions. An industrial section had hardly developed, and as such it could hardly aspire to play an independent political role.

Owing to its economic dependence on the British, its isolation from the people, and also from a belief in the fundamental goodness of British rule and British culture, this section could hardly assume the leadership of the movement. It was also afraid that the revival of the old order would jeopardize its position, and give a set-back to the plans of social reform. They felt that British rule was too well entrenched to be got rid of by these methods. They also lacked the necessary discipline and the capacity for organized action displayed by the "mutineers." While the middle class hardly counted in the North-Western areas, its influence certainly helped to keep coastal areas around Calcutta, Bombay and Madras largely free of anti-British out-bursts. It thus created a psychologically more favourable atmosphere round these areas for the British to plan their counter-attack. On their part, the "mutineers" treated Banias and Bengalis as hostile, and were definitely suspicious of all English educated persons.

The feudal class, too, was not a unified section. Its natural leaders, the Princes, though restive and suspicious of British policies, regarded any attempt to expel the British by force of arms as suicidal. Their spirit of independence had been crushed, and they desired only to be left in peace. Hence, neither the great Maratha princes, nor the Sikh rulers, nor the Nizam joined the rebellion. Their adherence could have made a vital difference. The siege train to Delhi could have hardly been gathered without the support of the Sikh princes. The English Commandant at Agra wrote frankly, "If the Scindia comes in, I shall pack up tomorrow." The loss of Agra would have driven the British forces to Allahabad and beyond. If the Nizam had come in, the whole of south India would have been aflame.

Thus, the leadership passed into the hands of disgruntled members of the old order such as Nana Saheb, the Rani of Jhansi, the Emperor Bahadur Shah, Kunwar Jagdish Singh, and some of their immediate dependents. The zamindars of Awadh joined after an order had been issued resuming their states, Elsewhere, the zamindars utilized the situation to try and regain their lost lands. Despite individual acts of great heroism such a leadership could not lead the popular movement to success. It could only think in terms of a revival of the old order—the very state of things which had paved the way for the British conquest of India. It would not thus be correct to compare the Uprising to the highly organized and conscious national movements of a later day. A unified India could hardly have emerged from the movement. If a comparison must be made it would be more correct to compare it with the Boxer rebellion of China in 1890. Both movements indicated the growth of powerful anti-British sentiments among the people, but neither could rise to the stature of full-fledged national movements.

CONSEQUENCES OF THE MUTINY

The establishment of a government of the "mutineers" in Delhi for even a limited period sharply posed the question of the forms of future political organization. It seems that discussions on these topics had been taking place even earlier at such places as the Arabic College, Delhi. Maulvi

Fazl-i-Haq Khairabadi, a noted divine, drew up a constitution for the government of the country.[2] The Court of Administration set up at Delhi, sometime in May, had a Council of 10—6 representing the army, and 4 the civil administration. The representatives of the army were to be "elected" — 2 each by the infantry, cavalry and artillery. It set definite rules for debate, and motions were to be passed by a majority vote. Without the approval of the Court and the President of the Court (who was appointed by the King), the King could not issue any order.[3] Thus, tentative efforts were made towards a limited monarchy. It was further realized that such a monarchy must be broad-base on the support of Hindus and Muslims alike, and must adopt a secularist approach. Bahadur Shah sternly forbade the slogan of Jihad and an Islamic state, saying, 'The Jihad is against the English, I have forbidden it against the Hindus'. He also issued a proclamation on the occasion of Id, prohibiting the slaughter of cows, buffalows, etc. "On pain of death and being blown up from a gun."[4]

If rebel rule has spread and lasted longer, these progressive features might have become stronger. But it is obvious that the Princely States would have opposed the slogan of a unified limited monarchy for the country under the aegis of the Mughal Emperor. In fact the fear against such a development was so strong that the Emperor's wife and even some of the close advisers of the Emperor maintained secret contact with the English all along.

Thus, the feudal class was neither unified nor consistent in its stand.

One of the most important political consequences of the Mutiny, was the shattering of popular faith in the old ruling class. The "treachery" of the princes rudely shook the faith and the consciousness of the people; they thenceforth

[2]See *Saurat-ul-Hindia* (Arabic), said to have been written by Maulana Fazl-i-Haq in the Andamans. Urdu translation by A.S. Sherwani from Bijnor in 1947, with a forward by Maulana Abul Kalam Azad.

[3]Press List of Mutiny Papers, 57, Nos. 539-541

[4]Press List p.111 S (31).

knew that they had nothing to expect from them. The other sections of the feudal class also proved themselves as impotent. The masses, therefore, slowly moved away from them and the British furthered this process by consciously making the Princes and the landed aristocracy the main social base of their rule in the country.

Simultaneously with the definite inauguration of the policy of preserving the princely states as political anachronism and "breakwaters" against a new popular uprising, an effort was made to attach the landed interests to the British power. Lytton wrote in 1876 to the Marquis of Salisbury, "I am convinced that the fundamental political mistake of able and experienced Indian officials is that we can hold India by what they call good government.... Politically speaking, the Indian peasantry is an inert mass. If it moves at all, it will move, not in obedience to its British benefactors, but to its native chiefs and princes, however, tyrannical they may be.... To secure completely and efficiently to utilize the Indian aristocracy is, I am convinced, the most important problem before us. Fortunately, for us, they are easily affected by sentiments, and susceptible to the influence of symbols."

With brief interludes, the policy of Lytton continued to form the main basis of the British administration of India for the next fifty years.

IMPORTANT DEVELOPMENT

The position vacated by the feudal classes was gradually acquired by the middle classes. By the seventies Lytton inveighed against the "Baboos ... who really represent nothing but the anomaly of their own position." The change in the position of the middle class from a position of loyal support to one of opposition is one of the most important political developments of nineteenth century India. It required the shock of the Mutiny to accomplish this. For it destroyed once for all the moral prop beneath the British government. The nakedness of a foreign domination based on force rather than the consent of the governed was laid bare for all to see. British military prestige also received a serious blow. And protestations of the rule of law, of democracy, and of Christian humility wore thin from the lips of those who had conducted a savage race war in which innocent men, women and children were brutally hunted down. The ferocious tirades of the Calcutta Press against all signs of what it considered a "soft" policy to the natives was a further shock. The educated classes began dimly to realize that they could never cross the barriers of race and colour, and started to seek affinities with their fellow countrymen.

A Factor Overlooked

The mortification and deep sense of humiliation at the failure against a handful of Englishmen, the savage treatment meted out by the British to old and proud families, the heightened racial arrogance of the victors, and a sense of common suffering also provided a psychological bond which marks out the Mutiny as a starting point for the growth of Indian nationalism. This is a factor which English historians often overlook. Long after its end, the events of the Mutiny continued to be discussed with bated breaths in the lanes and villages of India, and became the starting point of a new and different effort to oust the English.

Economically, the chief consequence of the assumption of direct responsibility for the government of India by the Crown was to facilitate the flow of British capital to India. The boom in the building of railways and the great irrigation works in North West India could scarcely have been carried out under the aegis of a private trading body. Apart from other results of this development, it powerfully aided the growth of an Indian bourgeoisie.

THE GAP WIDENS

Socially, the chief effect of the Mutiny was to drive the English and the Indians further apart, and to make the aristocracy more servile than ever. Favouritism, which was indirectly encouraged by the British—reached such absurd lengths that it made all decent minded Englishmen disgusted, and lowered Indian character in British eyes. From this point of view, the second half of the nineteenth century is one of the most depressing in the social history of modern India.

CULTURAL CRISIS

The disappearance of the Courts of Delhi and Lucknow left a big void in the cultural life of North India. Not only were these Courts the school for manners and morals for the upper layer of the society, they also had done much by their patronage to keep alive music and dance and to foster literature and other arts and crafts. The acute crisis of the feudal class following the Mutiny led to a deeper crisis that had been slowly developing since the British conquest of Bengal. Men like Raja Ram Mohan Roy had realized the nature of the challenge represented by the British, and had posed the problem of remodeling Indian society and culture. But a realization of the problem was not general—the old order was too deep-rooted and still held sway over the minds of men. By shaking the old order to is roots, the Mutiny made people painfully aware of the inadequacies and insufficiency of that order. On the other hand, those who stood for western values and western civilization became even further estranged from the people. Thus, the ground was prepared for the growth of broad movements aiming at the revival and regeneration of Indian society. The Muslims had not till then begun the process of adaptation to the new, as the Hindus in the coastal regions had already started to do to some extent. Mughal culture had, to a very large extent, become the accepted culture of both the Hindus and Muslims in the upper sections of the society in North India, and had also powerfully effected the upper sections in parts of South India. The failure of the old ruling class created a mood for rejecting the culture associated with them, i.e, the immediate past. Many sections sought to find in religion a means of reviving and re-vitalizing Indian society. Thus, they turned away from an oppressive and intolerable present to a glorified past.

Cultural revivalism and emphasis on religion as a means to social and political regeneration posed anew the problem of Hindu-Muslim relations. Men like Sir Sayyid Ahmad Khan sought to create among the Muslims an awareness of the needs of the times, and to reconcile Islam to the spirit of western civilization. The Arya Samaj attempted the same thing, with a more definitely revivalist emphasis. There were other trends too. The British attempted to exploit this situation to their advantage by systematically playing up the differences between the two communities. They also refused to countenance any proposals for social or institutional reform till there was a clearly expressed and overwhelming demand for them, thus giving a whiphand to the reactionary and orthodox sections in the two communities.

Thus, the "Mutiny" is not only the starting point of important political tendencies which have shaped the destinies of Modern India. It also posed clearly the fundamental problem of replacing the old feudal society and culture—not by a copy of the western society and culture, but by something rooted in Indian history and traditions and suited to the needs of the times. While many problems of this transformation have yet to be tackled, the entire social, economic and cultural development of Indian society during the past 100 years points to the Mutiny as the great watershed dividing modern India from the Medieval.

CHAPTER XI

Higher Education in India in the 70s and 80s and Social Change

Nehru was a man of many parts. He was not only a maker of modern India, but was deeply interested in all aspects of life including education. In his writings, one of the aspects which strikes one is his perception of the close link between education and social development. Deeply conscious of the progressive role the university system can play he warned the Universities against becoming "a home of narrow bigotry and petty objectives," and advised them that their scope of activities must ever enlarge if they are to play their full role.[1] Thus, he was far ahead of his time in conceptualizing the role of Universities. His warning against succumbing to narrow bigotry is even more apposite at a time when the forces of communalism and regionalism seem to be on the offensive in the country.

Foreign policy and education are two subjects on which everybody has an opinion. This would be welcome if the views were based on knowledge and understanding. Unfortunately, most of the views are either based on prejudice or on outmoded thinking unrelated to the existing reality. Much of the criticism also stems from the expectation that education would be the prime agent for social transformation, ushering in some kind of an egalitarian society, based on justice. The expectation that education would be the harbinger of social equality was, of course, not peculiar to India. This was an

[1]Nehru, Address at Allahabad University, December 12, 1947.

expectation, over the years, in the United States of America. The early Americans kept on emphasizing and believing that somehow or the other, through education they would be able to establish an egalitarian society. The dissipation of this rosy expectation is reflected in the writing of Howard R. Bowen, Chancellor of the Clemen University, who says:

"There is no assurance that progress towards equality of opportunity in any way would lessen inequality of condition. Equality opportunity is a worthwhile goal. It would enhance fairness in the contest for social position and it would improve efficiency by placing talent where it is most productive. But it would not significantly lessen inequality of condition. It would only re-arrange the population."[2]

One need not necessarily agree with this appreciation. What is missing here is the link between growth of education and simultaneous efforts in other branches of life in establishing an egalitarian society. In other words, one way of refusing to establish an egalitarian society is to put the responsibility for its success or failure on education, and not conduct an all-round struggle for such a new social order.

The question of the link between education and social change has been related by many thinkers to national traditions. The Edgar Faure Report, *Learning to Be* has some penetrating remarks on the subject. Categorizing efforts linking education with social change into three or four ideologies, the Report dubs the tradition where education was supposed to be for itself "the voluntarist" approach. It is this approach which is the dominant thread in the Report of the Education Commission. The Edgar Faure report says:

"Voluntarism consisting in the conviction that education can and must change the world, independently of any changes which may take place in the structure of society." (p.56).

[2]*Third Century*, p. 91.

The Education Commission Report headed by Dr. D.S. Kothari, says, "If this change on a grand scale is to be achieved without violent revolution (and even for that, it would be necessary) there is one instrument and one instrument only that can be used—EDUCATION." (p.8)

One may agree with the Edgar Faure Commission's remarks that "Education being a sub-system of society, necessarily reflects the main features of that society. It is vain to hope for a ... society woven out of privileges and discrimination developing a democratic education system."

The Kothari Education Commission's expectation that somehow if we invested adequately in education, we would be able to transform society peacefully was, to some extent, a legacy from the National Movement which accepted the ideal of an egalitarian society or Ram Rajya, but gave little thought to the mechanics of realizing it.

The Report of the Education Commission suffered from a number of other weaknesses too. J.P. Naik who was closely associated with the Education Commission Report, has, in his recent book, *The Education Commission and After*, tried to analyse why many of the major expectations of the Education Commission were not fulfilled. He has rightly noted that politically the position after 1968 was an extremely difficult one, so that little effort was made for some time to implement even those of its recommendations accepted by Government. But above all, Naik underlines the fact that the Report was written in a kind of a vacuum, the link between education and what might be called the "socio-political" reality being largely absent.

However, the Education Commission's Report, in many ways, was important for the growth of education in the country. It was the first Commission which was asked to, and took a comprehensive view of education. The Commission spent a lot of time in trying to understand the reality on the ground as it existed in different parts of the country and, in the process, elicited the opinions of a very large number of peoples. The Report made valuable suggestions, and I have no hesitation in confessing that during my tenure in the University Grants Commission, I leaned heavily upon it.

But I think that Naik had some justification in making the point that the Report became too massive and, in consequence, was unable to focus attention on key issues. The Education Commission Report tended to be treated by many sections as a type of a cafeteria from which one could pick up those aspects in which one was interested, ignoring the rest. For instance, as far as the teachers were concerned, they placed emphasis on revising the salaries and, in general, raising the position and status of teachers. They laid little emphasis on the problems of raising standards, or of making education more relevant to national development. The question of Major Universities, common schools etc. also acted as red herrings, so that the laudable effort of establishing a link between education and productivity and the EPR (Education, Productivity, Research) formula put forward by the Commission never made an impact on the Universities or the Government. The Education Commission also made a major point when it emphasized that education was not the business only of those concerned with teaching, or in preservation and transmission of tradition and values or the growth of individual personality, but with everyone, since education could not be delinked from the development of the nation, or from national productivity. This implied involving in the educational processes large numbers of those who had skills but little formal education. Potentially this was a revolutionary concept which could have bridged the gap between literary elites and skilled workers. Unfortunately, it was accepted only in words.

The first priority of the Education Commission was to effect structural changes in our system of education, second to raise quality, and third to regulate quantitative expansion of higher education—priorities which were the reverse of popular attitudes on the subject. It would be fatally easy to argue that none of these objectives or priorities have been realized: that despite quantitative expansion the structure of our educational system is basically the same as we inherited from the British; that quality has not risen, but, to a large extent, fallen; and that the question of regulating admission to secondary and higher education, either on the basis of merit or needs, has been talked about but never found politically acceptable. The question is: did we move in the desired direction or away from it? In other words, are we bemoaning that our progress was too slow, or that we are moving in a direction other than the one we proclaimed or desired?

My own conviction is that despite all difficulties and limitations, a strategy of maintaining, if not raising quality and, at the same time, preparing the ground for the transformation of the educational system in the country had been gradually hammered out. The strategy tried to combine attention to equality of opportunity with maintaining and raising standards, and preparing the ground for transformation of the educational system. An important plank was to make the universalization of primary education genuine, i.e. not merely on paper but in practice by enabling children from the poorer and deprived sections to stay on in schools by providing them mid-day meals, uniforms, text books etc. Simultaneously, an attempt was made to transform the rather rigid school system with its single point of entry to one where children could join in at various levels. Although the idea of non-formal education was accepted in principle, it was resisted in practice so that the attainment was much less than what might have been expected. However, the attempt to break the old mould and of trying to move in a new direction was important. The limited success was due not only to rigid attitudes, but also because there was in the country at that time a great deal of discussion whether the primary emphasis should be on the goal of universalization of primary education or on adult literacy. Politically, the goal of adult literacy appeared to be more attractive. However, it was felt that a massive programme of adult literacy, unless it was undertaken as a vitally important political campaign, would degenerate into an expensive bureaucratic exercise beyond the means of the country, and one which would erode programmes of universalization of primary education and the development of quality programmes at the higher level. Hence, a two-pronged approach was adopted. While the primary emphasis would be on the constitutional obligation of universal primary education, the programme of adult literacy was to be pursued with the help of students and unemployed educated people in the villages. Attempt also was to be made to involve mothers of young children in the programme. The use of students, it was hoped, would be less expensive and would not only help the poorer students to meet the cost of their studies but would enable students to have a better idea about the life and conditions of the weaker sections.

A second plank in the programme was of trying to bring in, on a selective basis, the poor but talented children into the educational mainstream. The idea was of setting up pace-setting or selective schools at the block and district levels where such students could be admitted. This was an ambitious and expensive programme where the support of the State Governments was necessary. That is why it could not proceed far. Nor was the Planning Commission prepared to find funds for such a programme in the Central sector. The expansion of the Central Schools was however to a considerable extent in response to this demand. It was accepted that it was not possible to establish quality or provide for justice to the weaker sections when they were on the verge of entering the colleges or the specialized institutions. Such as effort would have to be made at the primary and secondary levels, and this could only be done if quality-level schooling was available to the poor and talented children at all levels. Perhaps we would have been able to move in this direction faster if education had been put on the con-current list earlier than 1976 when the political situation in the country was different.

The third plank was of vocationalization at the secondary school level, simultaneously trying to reduce pressure on the colleges, and having a uniform system of education in the country by adopting the 10+2+3 system. Somehow, 10+2+3 became the main focus of discussion in the country rather than the first two i.e. vocationlization and regulating admissions to colleges which were interlinked, but were much more the major problems. Thus, it appeared as if the major thrust was on establishing a uniform pattern of education by introducing the 10+2+3 system. The idea of upgrading the talent of the people by making science compulsory up to Class X was also lost. A great deal of emphasis had been placed by the Education Commission on basic science being taught up to Class X in order to raise the skills of the pupils. Thus, it was not merely a programme of vocationalization. Vocationalization, again, has become a very popular slogan, but extremely difficult to implement in practice, not only because the vocations which need to be taught vary from area to area and need careful district surveys, but also because vocationalization is much more expensive than the normal arts/science education. Above all, the attempt was to change the existing hierarchical structure and its attendant values. The concept of work-experience was meant to change attitudes, not to try and make education financially self-supporting. Thus, it was methodologically not the same thing as Gandhiji's concept of Basic Education, though both emphasized dignity of labour. Finally, at the school level, an attempt was made to create a greater social awareness through programmes of national or social service through Nehru Yuvak Kendras, Social Service League etc.

At the University level, the major emphasis was on raising standards in a selective manner through quality programmes such as revision of syllabi, the introduction of examination reforms, the various faculty improvement programmes such as College Science and Social Science and Humanities Improvement Programme, Summer Institutes, etc. The emphasis on strengthening the research capacities of the Universities was also a new feature. Earlier, the University Grants Commission did not itself provide financial support or backing for research in the Universities. So much so that scientific research was earlier funded with the help of the National Science Foundation, a U.S. body. Also, little attempt had been made to identify important areas of research which were relevant to the needs of the country. Bearing this in mind, after 1973, the programme of Centre of Advanced Studies was strengthened and diversified. Teachers' salaries were revised along with qualifications. Raising of standards, or at any rate, preventing their erosion, was seen to be closely related to the unplanned proliferation of Colleges and Universities. Some effort was made in regulating the establishment of non-viable colleges and the proliferation of Universities by amending the UGC Act. According to the revised Act, no institution was entitled to receive central financial support unless it is declared fit for the purpose by the UGC. It was quickly realized however, that such an amendment alone was not sufficient to stop unplanned proliferation. It was, above all, a political issue, closely related to the aspirations of the people, and the strong, widespread feeling that provision of higher education was important for upward social mobility of the weaker sections. In order that curb on setting up new colleges did not militate against the interests of the weaker sections, the UGC encouraged Universities to start Correspondence Courses, and to enable not only women and working people but anyone to appear privately by studying in their own time.

It is not my contention that the programme outlined above transformed the educational scene. But it is argued that on the basis of practical experience and drawing selectively on the Report of the Education Commission, a strategy was evolved, bearing in mind the social and political constraints, whereby the triangle of equality, quality and relevance could be squared as far as possible. It was realized that the task of educational transformation was not something which could be achieved overnight. It meant a long haul, during which conflicting claims and aspirations had to be reconciled. The situation then as now may be summarized as follows: what we suffer from is not so much lack of a strategy as limited means, a woeful lack of public understanding of the issues involved in education, and expectations of quick returns without adequate and careful investment.

During the Janata regime, although the strategy above was not discarded in words, it was so in practice. During the period, a great deal of emphasis was placed on the concept of adult literacy. Adult literacy is extremely important both for democracy and development. But wherever adult literacy has been achieved, it has been achieved as a result of a massive political campaign, and as a part and parcel of a process of social transformation. The Janata Government hoped to achieve literacy largely by using student power, and that too student power which was mainly located in the cities. Nice and facile slogans such as "each one teach one" ignored this reality. Not only were the literates in the city, and the illiterates in the village, the value system of the two was vastly different. To expect the city man or student to successfully teach the villager, and also to "conscientize" him was a typically city-inspired, naive scheme from above to be run and executed by bureaucrats.

The programme of adult literacy did not mean that the programme of universalization of primary education was discarded, but it was put in the shade by the massive outlay for the programme of adult literacy. Many committees were appointed, brave targets were fixed, and even more impressive financial outlays were projected. In one meeting of educational experts and bureaucrats, where the Prime Minister, Shri Morarji Desai, was present, the target that one hundred million adults would be made literate during a period of ten years was reduced to five years—despite the protests of many members present, without budgeting for a single extra rupee. Thus, the Adult Literacy Programme was made the plaything of populism.

Similarly, the entire concept of 10+2+3 was formally adopted, but in practice it was drained of its real content. In place of vocationalization and work-experience, a vague concept, "socially useful productive labour," was put forward. It should be noted that Gandhiji's concept of Basic Education was not accepted even during the Janata period, though in a recent book, *The Crisis and Collapse of Education in India*, Shri J.D. Sethi has made this to be crucial failure in India. He argues that if Gandhiji's concept of Basic Education had been accepted by Pandit Jawaharlal Nehru in 1947, the entire educational situation would have been transformed. Regarding the 10+2+3 system, the then Prime Minister, Shri Morarji Desai denounced it as "disastrous," even though the Education Minister and other agencies had the courage to differ from him. It was quite certain that in the situation, no real progress could be made. Nor was there any question of making science an important factor in social transformation. While preparing a new, revised educational policy statement, all the references to "rationalism" and "scientific temper" were carefully cut out. Thus, the link between education and productivity, and the link between productivity and science was lost. The greatest emphasis was sought to be placed on character-building. Unfortunately, by character-building was not meant rationalism, or a spirit of co-operation or entrepreneurship but merely ethical and moral education. Nor were the ethics sought to be related to the ethic of the socialist transformation of the country.

During the Janata period, the Universities were also given a low priority. In fact, just as universal primary education was counter-posed to adult literacy, both were counter-posed to higher education. This was reflected in a sharp slashing down of the funds earmarked for the development of the Universities in the Sixth Plan. To some extent, the Universities were saved from the adverse effects of this policy decision because the Fifth Plan continued till 1979 and the funds already allotted to the UGC for the development of the Universities could not be cut. Efforts were made to emasculate the UGC itself, so that the academic community no longer looked upon it as a policy-making body for academic matters. This was reflected in Government giving the UGC a "directive" to review its programmes. This was an unprecedented step. It was unnecessary because the UGC had always been in the process of reviewing its programmes. Also, the work of the UGC since its inception had already been reviewed by a high power Committee headed by Shri V.S. Jha. But quite apart from this unfortunate development, the entire understanding was that the task of transforming the educational system was a comparatively quick and easy task. In fact, Shri Morarji Desai declared that he would change the entire educational system in six months time. When asked for a plan, he said that it was for the UGC to work it out. The upshot was that the need for developing a strategy which would prepare the country for a gradual transformation of the educational system was jettisoned.

This was the situation which emerged at the end of the Janata rule. As a result, the strategy which had been gradually hammered out during the early seventies suffered a serious set-back. It does not seem to me that a serious effort was made even after the defeat of the Janata to retrieve the damage to the educational system caused by the Janata rule. At least, this is what appeared from the outside since there was hardly been any public debate about education till now (1984). Thus, Government did not announce any new strategy for the universalization of primary education. According to the Constitution, this target has to be realized by the year 1986. We are already at the beginning of 1985, and it is quite clear that this target cannot be achieved. If so, what are the alternatives, and the priorities?

As far as the question of 10+2+3 is concerned, it seems to have received renewed emphasis. Only recently, according to the newspaper accounts, in such an important and large State as Uttar Pradesh, the Committee of Vice-Chancellors had decided not to implement the 10+2+3 system, largely on financial considerations. The figure of 150 crores mentioned in the papers was wholly an unrealistic one, based on the wrong assumption that *every* undergraduate college would have to add a year. To make 10+2+3 viable, U.P, M.P, Rajasthan, Punjab and Haryana have to be brought into the system, and backsliding in Bihar has to be stopped. Also, vocationalization has to be given a big boost.

The financial difficulties of implementing this scheme at the University level would be much less if in the name of populism, every under-graduate college was not allowed to introduce Hons. Classes. Standards can hardly be raised if Hons. teaching is extended from Universities, and selected Post-Graduate Colleges to weaker institutions. Even the decision that science would be taught in all schools up to Class X and would be introduced in a phased manner has not been pursued for no time-targets have been laid down for doing so. What is even more disturbing is that the rate of the growth of higher education which, from a growth rate of 12 to 14 per cent per annum in the 50s and 60s had declined to less than 4 per cent in the 70s, and thus become manageable, being near about the growth rate of the economy, has begun to grow again. According to the UGC Report for 1981-82, the growth rate was 7.3 per cent. The growth rate for 1982-83 may be even higher. It may be argued that the decline in the growth rate of enrolment in higher education earlier was largely due to growing educational unemployment, financial constraints, etc.—a fact which was conceded in the reports of the UGC. However, the restraint was certainly influenced by the implementation of the 10+2+3 in many of the States, expansion of Correspondence Courses and Own Time Study. The situation can change when the nation's growth rate rises.

As far as the growth of Universities is concerned, more and more universities are being established in various States every year, even without the prior concurrence of the UGC. I do not think any statistics need to be given in this regard, Also, more and more colleges are being established every year, even though 50 per cent of the existing colleges are non-viable, according to the UGC Reports. On a rough calculation, while from 1976-77 to 1979-80, about one Arts. Science/Commerce college per week was being added as compared to two colleges per week in the sixties, in the two years from 1980-81 to 1981-82, the number has almost reached the earlier figure, the average being 97.5 new colleges per year. While our enrolment in higher education is much below international standards, even a much stronger economy than ours can hardly afford to expand the formal system of higher education in Universities and Colleges so rapidly, and yet to maintain standards.

A number of issues need to be high lighted for healthy growth. The strategy which had been developed in the early seventies is still valid, but needs some revision and updating. First, much greater attention needs to be given to a selective development of the colleges since 85 per cent of the students study in colleges. I use the word "selective" in view of the virtual refusal of the State Governments to heed the UGC's advice to put a moratorium on establishing new colleges except in tribal and backward areas. The argument is valid that in a competitive situation no college would try to do better if it continues to get grant-in-aid on the same basis as any other college. Unless State Governments are prepared to adopt a differentiated basis or scale for grant-in-aid, the colleges in general will not make efforts to improve or raise standards. Such an approach might appear to go against the idea of egalitarianism. It is crude egalitarianism to think that it would be wrong to give incentives for those who do better. A differentiated grant-in-aid code for giving incentive to colleges for raising standards implies some kind of a "gradation" of the colleges, whatever the name you use. The question immediately arises; who should do this grading? It can hardly be done by those State agencies which are responsible for disbursing the grants. Perhaps, a Central agency could rise above caste, communal and regional considerations. Such an agency or agencies would either have to be set up by the UGC, or work closely with the UGC. A Grading Council has been set by the UGC subsequently, also a scheme for grant for Colleges for Excellence. The UGC scheme of autonomous colleges or colleges Assisted for Intensive Development (AID) can hardly succeed without such a differentiated approach. The idea of having multiple course streams at the University level so that the better colleges can adopt more ambitious course, is also one which has to be seen in this context.

Secondly, it is necessary to review the functioning and role of the teaching and examining Universities which are responsible for standards, courses, etc. in the affiliated colleges. All these years, the University Grants Commission has deplored the setting up of more and more Universities of this type, and advocated the idea that at least one University in the State should be of a unitary type so that it could act as some kind of a pace-setting institution. The entire question of examining the role of the Central

Universities is also connected with this idea, since it was hoped that Central Universities in different parts of the country would help to raise standards and act as pace-setting institutions. Also, they could also function as national institutions.

Leaving aside the Central, and a few State level unitary Universities, the standard form of the University system in our country is the Affiliating University. The structure and forms of these Universities need to be examined carefully. The experiment of the College Development Councils instituted by the UGC during the Fifth Plan in order that the Universities themselves plan the academic and general development of their affiliated colleges has, I am constrained to say, largely failed. The type of endemic "civil was" between the Faculty located in the colleges and the Faculty in the Teaching Department of the Affiliating Universities is one which has to be lived through to be believed. The Teaching Departments of the University are not looked upon, nor do they consider it their responsibility to help raise standards in the colleges. The Colleges are either regarded as rivals to the Teaching Departments, or a nuisance and a drag which prevent the teaching Departments to come up to their peers, i.e. other Universities in the country and abroad. The teachers in the old established colleges resent the superior airs of the teachers in the Teaching Departments. And thus it goes on. I sometimes wonder whether, just as High School and Intermediate Boards in various States have relieved the Universities of the burden of conducting the examinations, a solution could not be found by setting up similar Boards for the conduct of under-graduate examinations in the colleges. Once this responsibility is taken away from the University, it can perhaps pay more attention to the raising of standards, and post-graduate teaching and research.

Finally, the basic question of implementation: how do we implement programmes? Rather, the question is: what are the agencies of change available to us? For a variety of reasons, the organized teachers' movement in the country has not played a positive role in the task of raising standards or of trying to transform the present educational system. On occasions, the students have been found to be more in tune with the ideal and needs of the transformation of the educational system than the teachers. The teachers have vested interests which the students do not have. I would not say that the students do not have their own vested interests. They do have their own vested interests, but they are of a different type, and are not as well entrenched as those of the teachers. Thus, in reforming the syllabi, changing the educational system, introducing supplementary vocational courses, etc., the students have been found more responsive than the teachers. However, making the students responsible for transforming the system has its own dangers; it can lead to populism and the ultimate lowering of standards. Experiment in "total revolution" made by Jayaprakash Narayan and its failure shows the limitations of such an approach.

As far as political parties are concerned, it might have been expected that the Left and radical parties would have given greater thought to the question how the educational system in the country could be transformed and made to play a more positive role in the process of social change. Unfortunately, there has been a tendency to think that the first issue was to democratize education, and that this implied the transfer of authority, to the extent possible, to the hands of the students. It was not realized that the students themselves had definite class origins. Nor could they be considered more democratic than members of the Assembly and Parliament who had been elected by the people. In other words, in a country where election was based on adult franchise, the voice of the elected representatives of the people has to be considered more democratic than the voice of the students drawn from middle and lower middle classes.

So, we come back to the role of the political parties. It may be seen that in the election platforms of the radical parties, education figures only marginally. J.P. Naik's remarks on the rule of Government are germane. He says,

"... the political parties have generally remained ignorant of basic educational problems and take little interest except in such things as transfers, opening of new institutions, admissions, or grants (i.e. issues mainly dealing with patronage). The educational bureaucracy is on the whole weak and is unable either to formulate policies or to implement them. There have been, therefore, few pressures on Government from within to undertake and implement radical educational changes. Unfortunately, even pressures from outside have been non-existent. Of course, all interested groups have agitated, every now and then, for their individual or group demands. In fact, such demands have been almost continuous and Governments have been reacting to them in one way or another. But there have been no pressures or demands for radical educational reforms as such. There are no agencies in the country for whom "education" itself is a constituency and for which they are prepared to fight."[3]

Thus, no political party considers transformation of education as an important objective, though there are eminent individuals who feel concerned. As far as the Education Ministers are concerned, they very often have not been political heavy-weights, and hence unable to implement what they considered to be desirable. The situation was worse at the State level. There is no expert body at the State level. State level Grants Committees, framed on the model of the UGC, have not always played a positive role. State Grants Committees, even though they may be headed by eminent academics, have not looked at the educational scene bearing in mind the requirements of the nation as a whole. Differences regarding educational priorities between such bodies and the

[3]Education Commission and After, p.198.

UGC have often acted as an additional complicating factor. Setting up regional branches of the UGC have been suggested as a way out of this situation. I can understand the utility of such bodies if their primary role would be one of monitoring in which the UGC is woefully weak, and providing advance information which would be useful for planning (not dead information which is generally a couple of years out of date, and is useful only for adding weight to the Annual Reports, and providing data for future researchers). Co-ordinating Committees of Vice-Chancellors of the Universities located in the States, with adequate statistical and expert advisory services, and in which the UGC had due voice and representation could play a useful role. But the most important factor might be the strengthening of the Directorates of College Education by delegating to them the responsibility for planning the development, location, etc., of colleges, in consultation with the Universities. They could also arrange for the under-graduate examinations in affiliated colleges, as I had argued earlier. If necessary, this could even be done on a regional basis.

It is obvious that merely the device of strengthening central agencies such as the UGC, without at the same time strengthening the machinery of educational planning and monitoring at the State level will not provide in full the levers needed for transforming the educational system and making it an instrument for social change.

Apart from this, the role of an informed and enlightened public opinion is also important in a democracy. Of course, such an opinion cannot have any immediate or short-term results. It can only operate in the long run. Unfortunately, in our country, there are very few avenues whereby such a public opinion can be built or can express itself. Even in the university system, the attitude towards education is not very positive. Education Departments do not have a high priority, or high academic prestige in most of the

Universities. Hence, large educational issues do not really figure in educational debates in the Universities, and with analogous institution and institutions of National importance. An informed public opinion about education, especially higher education, can be developed once the Universities consider this to be one of their important, and not merely a marginal, concern. In other words, the task of building an informed, intelligent public opinion implies building a body of opinion which does not look upon education itself as marginal in our development. There is a danger that the idealism inherited from the national movement of making education an instrument of social change is being steadily eroded. If we do not link education to development, or conceive of education as an instrument of social change, it is not that the educational system will collapse but it will have an impact on our ethos. We are fond of using big words like crisis and collapse. What will happen, and is happening, is that education is becoming more and more the instrument of a narrow group in the ruling class to maintain the *status quo*. Disparities within the system are growing. People who have money and power have access to good institutions for their wards. The poorer and the weaker sections have no option but to be satisfied with poor, sub-standard institutions. This not only leads to social tensions, but means slower progress. In an era of rising expectations, growing disparities and slow economic and technological progress can only be a road to national disaster.

Thus, the question of linking education with social change is crucial for our national development, and cannot be set aside, or given up. Two points, however, have to be steadily kept in mind. First, that the process of educational change is generally a slow process. In our country, such a process has necessarily to be linked to the larger process of change in the country. Second, in view of the fact that the processes of educational change are little understood, and do not have a high priority with political parties, or even with the organized Teachers' Movement, the Universities and analogous bodies will have to come forward and make the question an important part of their programme and act as vehicles for educating public opinion. Just as national defence cannot be left to soldiers alone, education cannot be left to educationists and to expert bodies alone.

CHAPTER XII

Fundamentalism—A Tool of Imperialism

Ever since the rise of Khomeni to power in Iran, there has been increasing talk of the rise of "fundamentalism" as a new force to be reckoned with. Taking a cue from Iran, Ziaul Haq proclaimed his intention of instituting *Nizam-i-Mustafa* or the Law of the Prophet in Pakistan. Similarly, General Ershad of Bangladesh averred his desire to convert his country into an Islamic republic. Nepal is already a Hindu Kingdom. Thus, the waves of fundamentalism seem to be pushing into India from all sides.

The first question to be investigated is whether "fundamentalism" is a new phenomenon, as some western commentators would have us believe? In other words, is it a part of a genuine religious revival—a reassertion of the fundamental human spirit against the growing commercialism and materialism of the western industrial-capitalist system, or even more fundamentally, a return to the simple religion of faith as a reaction against the intellectualism and cold scientific temper of the modern world?

It is clear that fundamentalism is a complex development and has many facets, some of which have an intrinsic mass appeal. That is what makes it so much more dangerous, for the popular aspects are susceptible to, and in the past have been exploited for reactionary purposes, i.e., against the interests of the masses themselves.

Two aspects of religious revivalism which has figured in history need to be distinguished from each other: first, a religious protest against the harsh realities of life faced by the masses—exploitation, social discrimination, injustice, etc., and, second, a doctrinal assertion that the condition of the masses and the classes can be improved if the old faith and practices, based on egalitarianism (in fact, on a simpler less segmented social order), can be revived. The two aspects can be combined, but generally one of them plays a dominant role. Of course, a movement can pass from one to the other, either due to internal factors, or the impact or manipulation of external agencies.

It will be readily seen that protest against an unjust, exploitative economic or social system has within it the germs of a radical, even revolutionary movement, whereas the doctrinal, revivalist aspect trades on the ignorance and credulity of the masses. Protest against the unjust social system was voiced by the sufi and bhakti saints during medieval times, but the harsh social reality could not be changed without a clear-cut social philosophy. Hence, the doctrinal, revivalist aspect gradually became uppermost. In modern times, protest against the unjust colonial-capitalist system was voiced through various forms, including religious forms (i.e, the Brahmo Samaj, the Wahabi movement). A pan-Islamic movement in support of Turkey which can be traced back to the seventies of the nineteenth century was basically a movement of protest against the growing colonial/capitalist inroads of the West. However, Britain deliberately tried to turn it into a weapon against Tsarist expansionism, though they were all along conscious that it could, with equal facility, be turned against Britain, the leading colonial power in the world at the time. The manner in which British imperialism tried to turn a basically anti-Imperialist movement into an ally against its imperialist rival by using the *mullahs* and other agencies is a classic study in itself, and has many obvious parallels to the present situation. The interesting point to note is that this was the first time in India the *mullahs* were permitted, in fact, encouraged to use the mosques for what was basically a political movement. The Muslim "awakening" as it has been called, coincided with the Wahabi revivalist movement in India. The *Turkistan Gazette* (a Russian newspaper) of 25 May 1876, warned the British that if they sowed the wind of pan-Islamism, they would reap the whirlwind, and that England would have to repent later when the flames of Muslim fanaticism fanned by her would recoil on her. But the British were in no mood to heed such warnings. (R.L. Shukla, *Britain, India and the Turkish Empire*, Delhi, 1973).

Thus, neither fundamentalism, nor the attempt of Imperialism to use it in its interest are a new phenomenon. However, while revivalism was supposed to be a religious movement with political overtones modern fundamentalism is supposed to cover all aspects—religious, social, cultural, economic, and of course, political. Thus, it marks an accentuation of an old phenomenon.

A complex situation has risen with the collapse of the western colonial system following the defeat of Fascism in World War II. The well known Latin American political scientist, R. Stavenhagen, has summarized it in the following words:

"... post-colonial capitalist development produced large scale poverty by breaking up pre-capitalist modes of production and forms of social organization, furthering market economy and one-crop agriculture, uprooting people from their traditional villages, creating urban squalor and a growing landless proletariat. As the third world economies became increasingly incorporated into and subordinated to transnational capitalism, internal polarization and inequalities increased between social classes and regions."

This forms the background to the rise of fundamentalist movements in recent times. Two aspects of the movement may be noted. In those countries where there are no democratic forms of outlet, or where the ruling elites are seen as the defenders of an iniquitous social system and as the surrogates of western Imperialism, the movement assumes an anti-Imperialist, pro-people movement. Iran is the classic case of such a movement. But in a different situation, the ruling classes, with or without active Imperialist support, can use the discontent of the masses against the democratic elements. The first successful experiment of this type of a movement had been carried out in Indonesia at the behest of the C.I.A. in 1961 when in the name of Islam, Sukarno was removed, and a large scale massacre of the Communist and Left elements organized.

Nearer home, in Pakistan, the ruling class has often tried to promote fundamentalism in order to cover its denial of democratic rights to the people, in the process converting the country into a virtual colony of the U.S. Imperialists, and promoting a highly segmented, high cost society which was anything but Islamic. Also, fundamentalism in Pakistan is combined with an "ethnocratic" state in which one dominant culture, the Punjabi culture, tries to deny cultural rights to all other ethnic groups within the country.

Fundamentalism or religious revivalism has been at work in India for a long time. The Arya Samaj movement was basically revivalist, but since its dominant emphasis was on social reform, the doctrinal aspect was continuously whittled down. Both the R.S.S. and the Anand Marg were fundamentalists in the sense that they wanted a total reorganization of society or the old Hindu culture *as they saw it*. Both visualized multi-faceted action to achieve their objectives, including the training of a cadre dedicated to their objective. Neither believed in democracy, but were quite prepared to use democratic forms for the attainment of their objectives. While the Anand Marg was avowedly elitist, the R.S.S. sought to combine elitism with a mass cadre. Ideologically, the R.S.S. supported the idea of a Hindu nation.

Thus, a careful study of the growth of the national movement in India shows that there were, in the main, two basic philosophies which were struggling for mastery in India—one, the traditional philosophy which identified groups and persons on the basis of religion, race, caste, etc., and the other the concept of a new poly-ethnic or multi-national state in which religion, race, caste, etc., would play a secondary role. The former leaned heavily on the support of the traditional elites, the landed classes, the priestly hierarchy, etc., while the latter looked to the new industrial and professional classes, and then to the masses. The former trend was basically communal, fundamentalist and rigidly hierarchical, while the latter was secular, leaned on science, and was essentially democratic. While officially scorning the educated classes, derisively calling them "babu," the English instinctively realized that the greatest threat to British rule was from the latter. Thus, the British Home Secretary, Hamilton, wrote to Curzon in 1899:

"I think the real danger to our rule in India, not now but say 50 years hence, is the gradual adoption and adoption of Western agitation and organization...."

By agitation was meant political organization which implied democracy. The methods to counter this threat was also spelled out:

"... if we could break the Hindu educated party into two sections holding widely different views, we should, by such a division, strengthen our position against the subtle and continuous attack which the spread of education make on our present system of government."

Thus, the policy of propping up communal, fundamentalist groups and parties in opposition to the Congress and its secular approach to politics had been clearly set out as early as 1899.

While fundamentalism and secularism have always been seen as opposed to each other, the clash between the two has never been as deep as it is now. In a way it was inevitable. As our society prepares itself to move out of the old feudal mould, the contradictions between the new, emerging and the old, traditional forms become even sharper. The transition to a new social order implies a dual debate—among the protagonists of the new order whether the change implied merely the replacement of one hierarchy by another or a deeper change, and second, the debate between them and the protagonists of the order who use revivalism as their weapon. Thus, the process of change is not and cannot be a painless, or more or less a peaceful process. It is pregnant with conflict. This situation gives plenty of opportunity to interested foreign parties, to wit, Imperialism to intervene in order to delay, or disrupt the march of India to a free, self-sustaining entity, not dependent on Imperialism.

Once we discard the scenario of an easy, conflict-free, almost automatic transition to a new social order on the basis of gradual spread of education and filtration down of the fruits of economic development, a number of conclusions emerge:

(i) A sustained political—ideological struggle would be necessary to combat the poisonous ideology of fundamentalism and to work out the ideology and forms of the poly-ethnic, secular, democratic society postulated by the leaders of the national struggle for liberation. So far there has been a debate whether in the Indian conditions, secularism should mean lack of discrimination against all religious or equal respect to all of them. Nehru was clear that secularism did not imply disrespect to any religion, but that it was opposed to the fundamental approach of the leaders of organized religion towards the processes of social change. Speaking at the inauguration of the C.S.I.R. on 29 April 1950, he emphasized that "the scientific approach of life's problems was one of examining everything, of seeking truth by trial and error and by experiment." The religious approach, on the other hand, was "dogmatic," of asserting that this was so on the basis of scriptural authority.

Thus, whether we give respect to religion or not, a basic struggle in favour of the scientific approach and against the dogmatic religious-fundamentalist approach would have to be fought in all fields. There is no scope for compromise in this field.

(ii) Whenever the question of fighting communalism has been raised, we have been given a picture that if only a few communal books and passages were deleted from the school text-books, education would automatically become a major vehicle of national integration. While the exclusion of communal books and offending passages from school text-books is necessary and useful in itself, it will not thereby transform the educational system into an instrument of national integration. Communal and casteist educational organizations are being brought into being everyday, and communally minded or caste-oriented teachers appointed. Was this the intention of the founding fathers when they accorded religious minorities "the right to establish and administer educational institutions of their choice?" Since the government is committed to a drastic overhaul of the existing educational system, the manner in which it could be made truly secular needs careful consideration and debate.

(iii) Little concerted study has been made of the spread of the communal canker to even new areas. Is this in any way connected to lack of economic growth or its opposite, i.e., growth? In that case, should not our developmental strategy be re-examined from this point of view? Also, what is the physiognomy of the so-called "riot prone areas"? Perhaps, bodies such as the universities and other non-government organizations can undertake some action research on this point.

(iv) The questions needs to be raised: do our present political processes help, or are themselves a factor in the growth of casteism, communalism, fundamentalism, linguistic separatism, etc.? It is clear that neither the question of a code of conduct being accepted by the political parties, or defining communalism and on that basis, banning communal parties has made any progress. The A.I.C.C., in October 1961, had passed the following resolution:

"No place of worship such as temple, mandir, church, mosque, synagogue, gurdwara or headquarters of offices of a religious society or sangh or jamaat shall be used or allowed to be used for the purposes of political agitation or propaganda or for communal and anti-social activities."

The extent to which this resolution was implemented by the Government in letter and spirit is too well known for any comment.

Finally, on the basis of a report submitted by the Congress Committee on National Integration headed by Smt. Indira Gandhi, the Bhavanagar Session of the Indian National Congress (January 1961) had passed a comprehensive resolution, stating that the rise of communalism could be traced to political and economic developments which had released new forces and demands. *It was also linked to the working of democracy and the electoral system.*

In the '70s, there was some debate whether the Westminster system of individual constituencies was the most suitable to India, since it tended to give a premium to caste and communal considerations. However, the debate was sidetracked into a discussion between the Presidential and Parliamentary systems of government. Many European countries, such as F.R.G., Italy and France follow a modified list system as opposed to the system of individual constituencies. Should not academic bodies in India engage themselves in the pros and cons of such changes in India before a wide public debate can take place?

Thus, the struggle for secularism is an all-encompassing struggle and has to be waged by all healthy elements in our life, at the peril of remaining backward and dependent and even face national disintegration if we fail to wage the struggle in a conscious and consistent manner.

CHAPTER XIII

Religion and State in India and Search for Rationality

The purpose of this talk is to explore some aspects of state building in India, with special reference to the problems of secularism, the role of religion in state and nation building, and the question of rationality.

I do not, at this juncture, wish to raise the problem of nation or nationalism. At one stage, western thinkers identified nation with state. The British colonial rulers asserted that since India, unlike Britain or France—the basic points for reference for them, did not have *a single religion or a common language*, they were not a nation and, as such, did not qualify to exist as a state i.e. an independent nation-state. This, of course, was combined with the argument of backwardness of the peoples of the region, and the "civilizational mission" of the Whites. These arguments are, no longer put forward but the mentality behind them—of the westerners not being only different and superior, historically destined to dominate or rule over the rest of the world, is still reflected in much of the western treatment of the developing world.

The concept of nation and nationalism in relation to the newly independent countries or former colonies has, in recent years, been the subject of much debate in the west. The writings of Ernest Gellnar, Bendit Anderson, Paul Brass, Fukayama and Robert Haas are only a few of these. Many of the western scholars who were at one time giving lessons of nationalism to the colonial peoples, have now *discovered* that nationalism is not such a good idea. It is no longer considered to be the logical evolution of all history as propounded earlier.

It is argued that ethno-national identities are "contingent and imagined," and that "there was nothing inevitable about the rise of ethnic identity, and its transformation into nationalism." Fukayama, while conceding that nationalism was to some respects progressive, considers the quest of national identity to be "essentially a regressive phenomenon." Some western thinkers go so far as to dub national or ethno-national identity a deviation from individual moral choice into a relapse into a suffocating embrace of communal "embeddedness," an "escape from freedom," perhaps even a "pathological phenomenon."

It is not necessary for us to enter into this controversy here. Different peoples and societies have sought identity and means of bonding in different ways, nationalism being only one of them, though a significant one. Before taking leave of the modern debate on nationalism, I would like to underline that for many western thinkers, their basic precepts change sharply when they no longer seem to sub serve western interests. One may recall the period before the arrival of the Portuguese, followed by the Dutch and the English in Asian waters. They found in Asia a world where trade was by and large free and global, with only nominal—5 or 10 per cent duty being levied on imports. Arabs, Indians, Javanese, Malays and Chinese traded freely. The Portuguese, the Dutch and the English used their naval power to break this global free trade, and to establish their trading monopolies in the region. They used political and naval power to try to exclude the native traders from the global trade. When I was studying at the Allahabad University while the British ruled over India, their actions were not considered reprehensible. In fact, the Asian rulers were blamed for their inferiority in naval and military matters. Now, the same set of people from the West oppose the growth of national economies based on restricted trade opportunities, and advocate unrestrained globalization and liberalization. This has become the great western *mantra* which will enable all peoples, irrespective of their concrete conditions, to rise to their full stature if they would immediately implement it in full.

Again, I do not want to enter into the debate on globalization. My point is that ideas and concepts which originate in the west or any where else should not be accepted uncritically but, like all ideas, be examined carefully, and implemented if found useful, *bearing in mind specific, societal and historical traditions and conditions.*

We may in this context look at the concept of post-modernism which has become so fashionable in some quarters in the West and is being accepted almost as a gospel by some sections in our country. Central to this debate is the attack on secularism and on the post Renaissance concept of rationality. Thus, William M. McClay from the University of Tenessee speaking at the Wilson Centre pointed out that "These days it is more fashionable to be "spiritual" than to be secular." It has also been pointed out that the challenge to secularism was being mounted by "an intellectually sophisticated, and increasingly economical conservative religious counter-culture." This involved de-coupling of secularism from modernization since it is argued that a "progressive or modernizing agenda need not be a secularizing one." In fact, in some western academic centres, secularism's claim to universal truth and impersonal rationalism are decried "as a form of congnitive imperialism." This is on par with the neo-Marxist arguments put out earlier by some western scholars underlining the "objectively progressive role" of imperialism, in order to attack anti-imperialist national movements.

Moving away from this debate, and looking at our own traditions of the relationship between state and religion and pluralism, I would like to start by pointing out that the discussion about nature and objective of the state and its relationship with religion and society goes back in India several centuries before the Christian era. However, unlike Islam, religion and the state were not born simultaneously so to say. In India, the two developed separately and also interacted with each other. The celebrated work on state, the *Arthashastra*, ascribed to the Kautilya sets out the objective of the state as "to make acquisitions, to keep them secure, to improve them, and to distribute among the deserved the profits of improvement." In this context, *dharma* was considered one of the objectives, but given a secondary position. Although Buddhism considered *dharma* the central objective of state, and gave a higher position to the saint *(bhikku)* than to the supreme ruler *(chakravartin)*, the brahmanical thinkers merely advised the ruler to combine kingly duties *(niti)* with morality (*dharma*). This continued to be the Hindu view through historic times. In a general manner, the ruler was expected to maintain social stability. This was often implied to preserve the *existing* social order, in particular the four-fold division of the *varna* system, and respect of cultural pluralism by allowing people to pursue their own *dharma* or way of life. Thus, the final message to the king put forward in the Shantiparva of the *Mahabharata* was "Regard all religious faiths with reverence and ponder their teachings, but do not surrender your own judgement."

This implies that the state in India was never considered to be theocratic in nature. Nor could the state be considered Hindu (to use a later term) since kingly and religious duties were considered interdependent or distinct so that in some cases the ruler could even over-ride religious injunctions. This, with some differences, was in essence the Islamic concept of the state as it evolved in India.

As in the case of India during the early period, during the medieval period there was a lot of discussion in the

Islamic world regarding the nature of the state and its relationship with religion. The earlier idea of the combination of spiritual and secular authority in the hands of the Imam had come to an end with the rise of posts of Sultans in the 9th Century. The Sultan wielded only secular authority though efforts were made to raise their status by calling them *zill-allah* or shadow of God. They were duty bound to respect the *sharia* and honour the clerics, but they were answerable only to God. By this time Islamic society had become feudalized or hierarchical. The Sultan was duty bound to protect the existing unequal social order in the name of stability, as the *Siyasat Nama* of the Buyid, Nizam-ul-Mulk, shows. All that the ruler in such a state could do was to provide some succor and relief to the poor in the name of justice (*adl*), but these elements were to have no share in state power and were to be kept in their place by all means possible. Fakhr-i-Mudabbir and Ziyauddin Barani, the historian, writing in the 13th and 14th centuries, echo the words of Nizam-ul-Mulk. Barani says that the "low mean and ignoble" were "plentiful and abundant." They were not to be allowed a share in state power which would "disturb the high born people and lead the Kingdom to decline and fall." Any failure to put down these elements would lead to a breakdown in which there would be "complete community of women and property." These ideas were, in substance, echoed by Tulsidas in the 16th century, calling upon the powers that be to keep the *neech* which constituted the predominant section in society, under tight control.

According to many contemporary thinkers, a state based on *din*, or faith resting on social justice and morality had been abandoned once the rule of the Four Pious Caliphs (*Khilafat-i-Rashidin)* had come to an end. Going further, Ustad Ahmad Muhammad Jamal of Egypt maintains that Islam did not evolve any definite form of government. Nor did it lay down details for it. It only lays down some foundational principles of a generalized nature which do not vary with space and time and on which it is possible to build (a state) for the welfare of the people. Interestingly, even some modern Pakistani scholars are of the same view. Thus, Qamaruddin Khan, Professor of Islamic History, Karachi University, in his introduction to Al-Mawardi's *Theory of the State* is of the opinion that "the Quran does not aim to create a state but to create a society."

The historian Ziauddin Barani puts forward the concept that the state could only be based on *daulat* or *jahândâri* or worldly affairs, not *din* or faith. Akbar's friend and philosopher Abul Fazl put the ruler above all religious considerations, and strongly defended reason, denouncing *taqlid* or religious concepts based on rigid tradition.

Maulana Azad whose erudition as an Islamic scholar was accepted even by his opponents, never considered theocracy as an integral part of Islam, nor the rigid form of *sharia* which is considered by many ulama as the basis of an Islamic state, or the basis of laws of the state. He considered *din* to be the essence of religion, and *sharia* only its outer manifestation which changed with times and the situation. *Din* he considered "devotion to God and righteous living."

Maulana Azad's words are relevant in a world where forces of religious fundamentalism are rising all round us. It is significant that the deposed Indonesian President, Abdurrahman Wahid, who was himself a spiritual leader or *kiyayi*, lauded Azad's teachings when he visited India. He had declared: "Islam yes; Islamic state no."

There has been a considerable debate in India about the nature and meaning of secularism and whether it was a part of our tradition or an importation.

Nehru used the word "secularism" in the context first of struggle against religious obscurantism *which justified and sanctified an unjust and regressive social order*, and in the context of struggle for rationalism. Discussion has tended to concentrate only on the first aspect, viz. separation of state from religion. Nehru's vision has been objected to on the ground that all organized religions in Asia were maximalists—they considered religion to be an integral part of life, and divorcing religion, i.e. true religion from the state robbed it of its cultural ethos. According to T.N. Madan, secularism "was a stratagem, not a guidance for viable political action or *weltanchung*." Others argued that since mythologies and myth had a strong hold on the Asian mind, the secular struggle for rationalism was an impossible dream.

The present government (2001) has accepted the concept of "secularism" in words but its biggest partner, the BJP has robbed it of all its content by putting forward the concept of Hindutva, with their prescribed Hindu code of ethics forming the basis of cultural nationalism. This, in effect, denies the concept of pluralism which implied the emergence of a common national ethos without, however, attempting to erode or abrogate the cultural identities of different groups and religious communities.

Even more serious than their assault on pluralism is the attack on the concept of rationalism and humanism which, though a part of the Indian tradition, came to the fore-front in Europe in the post-Renaissance period, and was the basis of creating a separate sphere for science, away from religion. This was gradually extended to the fields of social science and culture. There has been much talk of introducing cultural values in our system of education. If by values is meant ethical values, such values were always an integral part of the school system. If, however, by values we mean religious values, it was always believed that the ethical and moral values propounded by various religions were essentially the same. Hence, there is a legitimate suspicion that in the name of value education, obscurantist ideas—some of them based on myths and mythology, would be promoted. It has not escaped anyone's attention that already a private T.V. channel is devoted to promoting all kinds of myths and legends in the name of culture.

That there is a definite attempt to undermine the rational humanistic tradition of the universities is made clear by the manner in which astrology and *karma kanda* are being sought to be smuggled into the universities. Natural scientists all over the country have made no bones that they consider astrology to be a pseudo science, like alchemy. If the government was keen only to promote the scientific study of astrology, as it claims, it could easily promote astrology in various institutions *outside* the university system. That introduction of astrology in the universities would be the thin end of the wedge to introduce all kinds of pseudo scientific practices was made manifest when I received an invitation from Professor Ram Krishna Sastri, designating himself as Vice Chancellor of the Viswa Jyotish Institute, Kolkata, to a conference next year where in addition to astronomy and astrology, palmistry, numerology, *vastu, tantra,* phsiognomy etc. would also, be discussed. It was claimed that the project had the moral support of the government of the country, that many Central and State Ministers, Supreme Court and High Court judges, Chancellors and Vice Chancellors of universities were expected to attend, and that the Prime Minister Shri Atal Bihari Vajpayee had expressed his willingness to inaugurate the same.

This shows how far we have come. That such a galaxy of persons are expected to attend a function which goes in the face of modern science and rationalism shows the atmosphere of pseudo rationalism that has been created. That too, at a time when the Planning Commission and the Government keep talking of making India a knowledge super-power based on modern science and technology and the information system. Can the building of a knowledge based super-power go hand in hand with undermining the rational, humanistic basis of the university system?

Regarding the revival of religion in the West, those who are a part of the movement also state clearly that taboos, superstitions, supernaturalism and irrationality were "vestiges of humanity's childhood," and for them religion is "an dispensable force for the up-holding of human dignity and moral order."

Unfortunately, such a distinction in religion between the supernatural and irrational elements and struggle for human dignity and moral order is not being made in our country. That is why Nehru's combination of secularism with struggle against obscurantism and caste based social distinctions is meaningful even today. Shri P.N. Haksar was not only a close associate of Nehru, but always lent his support against the forces of irrationalism and obscurantism. In remembering him, we should also pledge ourselves to continue his call for a rational and just social order, based on secularism, pluralism and toleration.

Index